JENNIFER L MOORE, LMFT

# Honest to God

*How a Lying Evangelical Became an Honest Lesbian*

*For Liza:*
*the sunrise at the end of my long dark night.*

# Contents

# 1

# The Right Stuff

"This song is a sign!" I declared to no one else in the car.

It was July in South Carolina. The sun was out, my windows were down, and "The Right Stuff" by the New Kids on the Block was blasting on my radio. It cooled the burning old lady vibes churning in my stomach as I pulled onto a college campus for the first time in 15 years.

I was ten minutes away from my first interview with the admissions counselor. Applying to get my graduate degree in Marriage and Family Therapy was both a dream I had long procrastinated and a hail Mary last ditch effort to be somebody. The past I had piled behind me was a smelly heap of humiliating choices and failed attempts to create a life of substance. Reflecting on my first 35 years seized my chest with regret for dreams not followed, embarrassment for choices poorly made, and shame for entanglements I had allowed. One simply should not be my age, renting a room from their brother, working for minimum wage and driving their mom's old car. Complete reinvention was the only solution that could fix this situation.

NKOTB brought out the kind of energy I needed to face the day. It was only an interview, but the electricity in the air signaled the possibility that some future version of myself might remember the moment as the first day of the best chapter of my life. First days are invigorating that way. A blank notebook fresh from the wrapper, free of mistakes and full of potential; powerful launchpads catapulting us into the unknown. They are everything that could be, anything you want and playgrounds for your wild imagination. Every year as a child I dreamt of returning to school on the first day completely reinvented. It was my fondest daydream to imagine boys' heads turning and girls' jaws dropping as I walked into school a fully grown woman. This was never so true as the first day of 9th grade.

Bangs. Temple to temple, above the eyebrow, every hair from my crown forward, chopped off in a perfect line to reveal my hazel eyes. No matter how I brushed it, or how I didn't, how I frolicked or played, ne'er a hair blocked my view. These bangs had been my mother's choice to frame my three year old cheeks and I hadn't ever considered changing. Why mess with a good thing? All around me, other girls graduated from the blunt bangs of elementary school for the White Rain feathered bangs of junior high.

Desperate to be a woman, I tried, God how I tried, to glue, fluff and paste my bangs to a proud attention. I'd pull my hair up high in one hand and use the black rat tail comb I stole from Dad's medicine cabinet in the other to feverishly tease it all down from my fingers, mimicking what I had seen other girls doing. Before those hairs knew what hit them, I would soak them up with cold, sticky hairspray. Briefly they stood, poised atop my head with pure glam, so punk rock.

"Noooo...dangit!" I cried quietly, watching them sag back down in slow motion, burdened by the weight of my gusto. A quick soap and rinse in the bathroom sink, blow-dry and try, try again until Mom's call pierced the morning air to announce the time. By her second, more impatient bellow, I had washed, rinsed, and dried out all of the product a final time. My eyes watered as I looked at my bangs in the mirror. They had crushed me with their tenacity to remain blocky, boring face-drapes. Becoming a woman was hard.

From classmates, I gleaned that being a woman meant full body obsession and complete intellectual neglect. Be thin, porcelain, and fluid. Do not be smart, loud, or brave. Your power came from the tightness of your body and majesty of your mane. Try as I might, I was no proper woman. Both my tummy and cheeks puffed plump and round. My clothes strained across my large frame, a state worsened by my constant tugging and pulling at their seams. My hair was flat, dense and lifeless.

The girl I met in the mirror's reflection was too nice to make fun of, but too plain to remember. By fifteen, my six foot frame towered over most other people, adults included. Invisibility rendered impossible, I attempted to remain hidden. I slouched or bent my knees to shrink, kept to the side of the room in class, and in the back of the pictures in the yearbook.

The pressure to fill out and blossom was heavy in the halls of high school. Panic flooded my chest at the thought of having to radiate the kind of luminescence that would draw handsome teen boys my way. Who might love this bumbling girl with bangs? I knew my family loved me. That felt like a given. All of the struggling to belong to the world outside of my home felt like a betrayal to the sweetness of my family. I felt almost like I had to protect them from the embarrassment of being associated with me and all my awkwardness.

Mom and Dad met and fell in love as teenagers at a roller skating rink in the late fifties. Theirs was a storybook kind of love that a kid can only aspire to find. To look at pictures of them, I felt sure they were A-list kids, wildly popular, rich and fabulous. They weren't. Mom's family was solidly blue collar, her dad a postal worker, her mom a homemaker and faithful church attender. Dad's mom also stayed at home as women in the fifties often did, but his dad died when he was a toddler. His mom remarried a growling over the road trucker who provided a decent life, especially when he was away.

Dad was a bit of a paradox. I have vivid memories of him being goofy and silly. He would tickle us and foot wrestle and throw us very high in the pool to make a splash. He would call me all manner of silly names like Booger-butt, Sugar-belly, Jenipers or Jiggers. My childhood is dominated by images of him in his blue bathrobe making chocolate-chip pancakes and whistling songs about warm woolen mittens. But he was also pretty stressed.

There were seasons of life when his worries furrowed his brow and silenced his whistle. He worked for a meat packing company that relocated him every year for several years and he just had to keep breaking our hearts with another move. We weren't rich people by any stretch and moving every year makes it hard to build equity in your investments. He loved saying yes to things we wanted, but there were just seasons where he could only say no. His stress lent to him having a short temper and spending some evenings growling to himself in his recliner. Even through his moods we knew he loved us. If he barked, he'd come back around and apologize. He was very good at drawing lines and I dared not cross them, partly for fear of his mad face, and partly because I never ever wanted to disappoint him.

If Dad drew the lines, Mom painted in the colors. She painted a lot of things, actually. The more we moved, the more she found the bright side by seeing each new house as a blank canvas for a whole new perspective. My mom can paint a wall better than any handyman I've ever met. She has always been good at making the best out of tough situations. She spent a great deal of care and energy cultivating a sense of home no matter what city we lived in. She would paint, make curtains, arrange and rearrange the furniture in every new house. Was she particular? Yes. Could we move a stack of coasters to the wrong side of the table and watch her unconsciously move them back? Yes! Did we love that about her? Yes.

Even when we were chaotic messy children our mom managed to tame the wildness of our home every day. She was also a master of creating comfort. When we got sick she was ready with ginger ale and humidifiers. We'd be quickly set up in our beds with wash cloths, thermometers, beverages and snacks to help us heal.

She was a quintessential woman. Every picture I saw of her reflected a girl of style and grace. And, she would point out, she made that dress she was wearing in the picture from her own pattern. I don't really know how much effort Mom put into looking as beautiful as she did, because she never made it a spectacle. It was important to look nice, but it was not a big deal and it was certainly not the most important thing about a person.

My big sister was much older than me. We only lived in the same house until I was about 8. She was always grown and exotic and by the time my brain started holding on to memories, she was a teen and had important things to tend to. She had a TI 99 plug-in computer in her room. It was a chunky keyboard with a cartridge slot on one side, and I would play primitive video games of spaceships shooting aliens, or mountain climbers side-stepping bears while she got ready. I'd steal glimpses of her meticulously drawing on eye liner, and would dazzle at the height and breadth she could achieve with her hair and a massive amount of Aqua-net. She had a purse, keys, and went to work in her car which made her a grown woman in my eyes.

My big brother was closer to my age, but still five years older, so my earliest memories of him are of playing together in my room. Because he was older, he could make toys dance in ways I couldn't and would create story arcs that dazzled me. Once my brother got too old to bother with me, I would be forced to find other ways to connect to him. When he wasn't home I would tip-toe into his bedroom. It always smelled of sour laundry and body spray. Maybe I was looking for secrets, clues to who he was becoming, or dirt I could leverage against him. Or maybe I had just read *Harriet the Spy* too many times and was becoming a sneaky little kid.

Mom and Dad were glad to be involved in our lives. They showed up to basketball games, and volunteered in the band boosters. We had family dinner every night and went to church together every Sunday. I had no reason from inside of my family to think I was letting anyone down, but as the youngest, I learned early to compare myself to everyone ahead of me. My world was packed with role models and I knew I was doing well if I could both follow in their footsteps and avoid the pits into which they fell. I tried incredibly hard to do both.

We were United Methodists. Engaged, compassionate, community minded, but not fanatical. Methodists went to church every Sunday, including Sunday school, but that was it. The rest of the week, the church was used by the boy scouts and girl scouts and maybe a group of recovering addicts.

On Sundays, we held sophisticated services with bulletins, acolytes, and pressed robes choreographed to perfection. Every service was a polished offering to a distant king. You knew when the service was starting, when to stand and when to read your parts aloud. The same services were held in the same order year after year in accordance with the cycle of holidays. It was predictable, comfortable, and maybe a little boring. You went because it's what people do and it helps make you a good person.

Being United Methodists offered a very stabilizing consistency. You could go to any United Methodist Church in the country and it would feel very similar. In every new city, we joined the church, got our picture in the directory and faithfully attended services. It was a part of our identity, but not the overwhelming sum of it. That is, until I broke the cycle.

# 2

# Jesus Christ

My finger traced the smooth finish of the mouse in my hand. My cursor hovered over the start button as I listened to the instructor give directions for taking the test.

"When you reach the last question, the prompt will ask you if you're ready to submit. Click yes. Your answers will be analyzed and a copy of your results will be sent to each school you listed on your registration. You will also receive a copy in your email in five business days."

The moment I had been procrastinating for fifteen years had arrived. I hate tests. Just the thought of having to take one increases my heart rate and dries out my throat. I am not good under pressure. Once in high school a teacher literally gave us a copy of the test with the answers. All we had to do was memorize them and regurgitate them and I still missed five. The idea that my performance in this moment would determine whether or not I got to pursue the future I desired was overwhelming at best. The only thing that cooled my burning test anxiety was Jesus. If I was meant to pass this test, then he would make sure I did.

"If God can lead me to it, He can lead me through it," I whispered to myself and clicked the start button.

I was re-born on August 13, 1993. It was my first full summer of living in a very small town in the foothills of South Carolina. This town had a population of around 1200, and a church count of 28. Small southern towns have such a high church count for two reasons: they really love Jesus, and they really hate each other.

A new school friend had invited me to the youth group that met at her Baptist church with promises of fun, snacks and an especially handsome youth pastor. I went for the snacks and to get closer to my friend. At the end of the first meeting, Handsome Youth Pastor made a pleading argument.

"We're about to wrap up our evening guys," he hushed his voice to a tender, reflective tone.

"I know some of y'all are with us for the first time, and I just want to tell you that Jesus loves you. He wants to spend forever with you and his father God in heaven. But we can't be close to God because we are tainted with sin. God can't be near sin. But I'm here to tell ya, Jesus Christ made a way for you." His eyes started to water and there was a catch in his throat.

"Jesus suffered and died on the cross for you so that your sins would be washed away and you'd be white as snow. Because of his sacrifice you can be with God in Heaven forever! If you want to know how to receive this gift of his, just come talk to me before you leave and we can make it happen. Sound good?"

A few teens clapped while others groaned their tired affirmations. He wished us goodnight and everyone filed out of the double doors back to their parent's waiting car.

I was gobsmacked. All these years of seeing Jesus depicted in bloody, sweaty suffering on the cross and, as it turned out, it was all my fault. I felt a swirl of guilt and gratitude. What selfishness it would be for me to say, "No thanks Jesus, I'll pass." Of course, I leapt at the opportunity to accept the offer of heaven. I approached the youth pastor and told him I wanted to go to Heaven. He was so delighted he got tears in his eyes and knelt with me next to a folding chair and led me in a prayer. Then he wrapped his handsome arms around me and told me he was so proud of my decision. It felt amazing. I officially belonged.

As a 15-year-old fresh convert I was deeply troubled and betrayed once I was enlightened to God's wrath and jealousy. Yes, the Methodists taught us that there was a place called Hell, and that monsters who deserved it would go there, but their list seemed very short, and it was never truly up to us to say who was on it. Until that year, it hadn't been conceivable that I would *ever* be Hell-bound. While this changed my idea of God in many respects, I still felt grateful to know. How special was it that God had directed my path right to this church, at this time, for this reason? As deep as my gratitude was penetrating, there followed a building anguish for the billions of souls who didn't know Jesus. I wondered how many would die before they heard what I had heard. I thought of countries full of Buddhists, Muslims, and Hindus bowing down to false gods and prophets and my heart just broke for them. Those poor lost souls had no idea what was coming for them. I simply had to do something to help them. I had to show people the way.

Mom and Dad found my spiritual awakening disorienting. We were Methodists, not meth addicts. From what did I actually need saving, choir practice? They drew tough boundaries around my church attendance. I wasn't permitted to go to my new church on Sunday morning: that was family time. Sunday night, Wednesday night and Saturdays were fine. When forced into the charade that was Methodism, I would roll my eyes and clutch my metaphorical pearls at the blasphemous things they said in Sunday School and from the pulpit. My Dad's eyebrows would furrow at me as I sighed and shifted in the pew next to him. I could only pray that my family would someday come to the light.

My new youth pastor approached me after Wednesday night youth group to remind me that new believers needed to be baptized when they came to a saving knowledge of Christ.

"Baptism is the moment you say to everyone, "I love Jesus and I'm proud of it!"" his eyes sparkled beneath his bleached and spiky hair.

"Um…yeah…I really wanna do that. Of course. I just have to get permission." I knew my parents would feel strange about this.

"No ma'am," snapped my dad, "You already got baptized as a baby in our church, you don't need to do it again. Why do you need to do it again?"

"I dunno," Dad's questions were always intimidating, "Pastor says baptism is done this way so it's like to die and come back to life again. He just told me I'm s'posed to."

"Well, you tell him you already have and that's that."

Mom wrung her hands, she was so uncomfortable. Guilt squeezed my stomach. Their faith wasn't bad, they were great people and they loved God. They were the purest hearted people I knew. Putting them through all of this stress was unnecessary. Anyone else who got saved also got Baptized and the Pastor was just trying to help me on the path. Honestly, the thought of splashing around a bathtub of water in front of hundreds of people was terrifying and embarrassing, Dad had protected me from that much.

His limitations didn't cool my tenacity. I continued going to my own church three days a week and investing in my relationships with God and others. My week revolved around youth group on Sunday nights.

Youth group was the most vital element in being a good Christian teen in the 90s. At school you'd get lost in the crowd, tossed about and squeezed into cliques. It was political and messy. In youth group you got to share your deepest struggles and support each other through trials. You were all facing the same dragon: standing out for Jesus. On Sunday nights, you belonged.

The youth room was lined with brown tattered couches and bean bags in the musty basement of the church. The brown paneled walls held posters of Jesus hugging drug addicts, and Noah's ark in a stormy sea. The youth pastor was captivating us with a sermon about self-sacrifice and choosing to separate ourselves from the world. We could be assured that persecution for being Christians would come for us. People who didn't know God would never understand what made us special and that would infuriate them. The Devil, however, was prowling around us using the world and all of its trappings to ensnare us in his grip. We had to be diligent. We had to be willing to die for Jesus. My heart raced with dread at the apparent inevitability of someone holding a gun to my head while questioning my devotion.

We were invited to reflect on our lives, examining ourselves for ways the Devil might be trying to influence us. Were we reading worldly books? Were we listening to worldly music? Would Jesus find anything that we consumed offensive or lacking? Shame washed over me. I did so many despicable things. I read books about teen girls kissing boys and being rebellious. I listened to heavy metal music. I read magazines about heart-throbs and had posters of Luke Perry on the wall of my bedroom. God must have been so ashamed of me.

One of the young men hoisted a clenched fist in the air and shouted, "We have to free ourselves from these things! Let's burn it all!"

The pastor's pride turned up the corners of his mouth. "That's a great idea, son. Let's do it. We will be ridding our lives of these strongholds and the smoke will show the world that we love Jesus more than anything it could ever offer us!"

We all cheered!

The bonfire was scheduled for Saturday. We could burn all of our sinful materials and then have a hot dog roast at the pavilion behind the church. Everyone was asked to bring their worldly propaganda and favorite kind of cookies.

The day arrived, beautiful and sunny. A light breeze convinced the tall grasses to dance in the field behind the sanctuary. The pastor lit a fire in an old oil barrel and stoked it to life with nearby sticks and twigs. In my arms I clutched a milk crate full of my most sinful artifacts. 90210 posters, Rolling Stone magazines and four CDs: Megadeath, Metallica, Pearl Jam and Nirvana. Other kids brought their own containers filled with books and CDs. Some kids included video games and comic books: evidence of their sinfulness. The pastor initiated the rite with a prayer.

"Lord, we come to you today with grateful hearts. Thank you for providing a beautiful day for us this morning. We come to you carrying these trinkets of the world, these temptations that bind us, these anchors of sin. We offer them up to you as a sign of our devotion to the narrow path, to your way." The pulse in his words lent a subtle tempo to his prayer. His voice swelling and relaxing in a hypnotizing rhythm. "We acknowledge we have been led astray by the lusts of the flesh and the sins of this earth and ask that you accept these offerings as a sacrifice to your name. Bless our hearts and direct our paths in Jesus' name! Amen!"

We mumbled a collective "amen" and then one by one dumped the contents of each of our boxes into the hungry flames. Black smoke poured upward from the barrel into the sky and up to the throne of God in heaven. The caustic smell of melting plastic and paper burned our noses. Flakes of ash fell like snowflakes onto our shoulders. Some people wept grieving their sins, or perhaps over the loss of their Red Hot Chili Peppers album. I stared coldly at the melting mass of filth, feeling the righteousness that only such boldness could invite. We were better than other kids. We were children after God's own heart.

My sense of belonging grew the deeper I stepped into Evangelical faith. My inner ugly duckling found a place for herself in the pursuit of modesty and purity. Scripture required all women to cover their bodies to shield the hearts of our brothers in Christ from wandering their eyes over her exposed flesh in lustful temptation. I was no longer covering up because I was ashamed of my imperfect body, I was protecting the boys. Purity was a sacred practice and it was imperative that we didn't let anyone trample on the flower of our virginity. Sex wouldn't be good until we were married. What a relief to explain to people that I was a virgin because of God's request, and not because of the lack of requests from interested parties.

Despite the passion of our pastor's heart on the matter, my church friends still seemed to be beautiful in worldly ways and kept in lock step with the high brow fashions of the nineties. Even worse, the boys loved it. Modest women were still wearing double tank-tops and had coppery dark tans under their rolled up khaki shorts. I felt sure they spent an inordinate amount of time giving themselves that effortless no-make-up look.

At a sleepover, my friends woke up early to start preparing for church. After I tossed a skinny strapped sundress over a T-shirt and ran a brush through my hair, I sat on the edge of the bed watching them pull, tease and feather their hair, then pluck, powder and paint their faces. Still just an eight year old in my sister's room.

"Are you ready already?" one asked.

"Um...yeah...I'm all set," I offered sheepishly, "I'm pretty low maintenance."

"Ugh, I wish I were. I can't even leave the house without make-up on, I would just *die!*"

A part of me wanted to make fun of them and write them off as looking stupid, or even sinful. But I also longed to be them and wished I knew how. It was such a sticky situation. Being beautiful was the path to acceptance, but God said vanity was wrong. My self-righteousness struggled to polish my fading self-esteem. Vanity was a terrifying place to me, but they struggled to resist its lure. Our differences would continue to pile up against me. If no one else in the world existed, I would be dirty in a pond somewhere watching the life cycle of frogs. But with all these girls around and their pressures, and all these boys and their desires, there was no room for frogs.

Trying as hard as I could and hoping to blend in was the middle path between total self abandonment and belonging. With this face, and these features, I accepted I wouldn't pull off glamour. All the primping in the world seemed a futile effort to evade the inevitable conclusion: I was not pretty like other girls. It was imprinted in their DNA, they were coded to eventually bloom into roses and I was not. I was a dandelion. Just a stumpy little flower straining from a crack in the pavement. Perfectly pluck-able. Nothing to see here.

# 3

# Divine Appointments

The murmur of browsing nerds hummed around me as I flipped through the short stack of self-help books I had brought to my table. Between sips of my latte I skimmed their chapter titles dazzled by how effortless they each made it seem to affect change. I have always been obsessed with self-help. Even as a kid, we would take family trips to the library and I would nestle a copy of "7 Habits" in my stack of teen fiction. Our mind's ability to influence our lives is so incredibly fascinating. It was my love of the power of thought that inspired me to be a psychology major in undergrad. Of course, whenever I told anyone I was a psych major, they took it upon themselves to warn me that you can't do shit with a psych degree unless you go to grad school. I heard them, I knew it, and it only took me 15 years after getting that psych degree to finally apply for grad school.

The first time it remotely occurred to me that I might want to be a therapist was after watching "Good Will Hunting" with friends in the dorm. I was mesmerized by the way Sean worked like a psychological surgeon, cutting through Will's bullshit and removing his infected inner demons as though they were a diseased gallbladder. My undergrad professors cooled my passionate aspirations with lessons from their own clinical work. They would recount stories of their battle against mental illness–grizzled war heroes at the Veteran's day cookout. With touches of hyperbole and their own secondary trauma they triggered enough self-doubt in me to suspend me in hopeless inaction for all those years. I couldn't imagine myself talking a man down from a ledge, drawing shameful secrets from a frightened child, or staring in the eyes of a murderer as he described his vicious killings. According to them, their jobs had required just such work on a regular basis. Though my heart longed for the path of psychology, my insecurity found a more hopeful path in spirituality, that's why I elected to be a double major in psychology and religion.

The years I spent marinating in the gospel before college did a great job of convincing me that I was weak and flawed. Baptist theology gave me the perfect structure for self-doubt, affirming my constant inner criticism. I wasn't just flawed, I was fallen. Christians around me often mocked the very idea of self esteem. You shouldn't *have* self esteem, you should only have Jesus-esteem. He's the only good thing about you anyway.

By the time I had enrolled, I had grown enough in my faith to realize that though I was deplorable, Jesus was the ticket to being cool. I had masterfully learned to overcome feelings of being an outcast with allusions of holiness. My conversation was tastefully seasoned with spiritual flavors, and the grape juice that had once been my shyness had aged into the wine of pensive wisdom. By my senior year, I was popular, funny, and it was a well known fact that I gave the best hugs, and most heartfelt notes of encouragement, scriptural references included. My insecurity was nearly totally eclipsed by my righteous humility. My relationship with God regularly rescued me from anything that without him, would have drowned me in shame.

The jury is still out as to whether or not I made a wise choice about college. There are lots of points to consider. But there are two things I have always felt were worth the crippling debt of a private Christian university education. The first was the small pond atmosphere that inspired and supported my anxiety-laden quest to be a musician and the second, but far more valuable, was Rosina.

In the late summer heat of South Carolina, freshmen were moving into the dorms. Sweaty both from the heat of the task and the absence of air conditioning in our rooms, I boarded the elevator to discover I wasn't alone.

Waiting in the corner stood a bubbly young woman, dressed in a red pocket T-shirt with the sleeves folded to reveal white cuffs, jean shorts rolled just so and red shoes that perfectly matched both her shirt and the red bow around her high ponytail. We made eye contact and she poked her hand out as she chirped, "Hi, my name is Rosina, but you can call me Ro, as in your boat!" Clearly pleased with herself she smiled excitedly waiting for my acknowledgement. I took her hand, unsure of what to say, and managed a "nice to meet you." We rode to our floor and I felt reasonably assured I could never be friends with a girl like her.

Childhood relocations quickly teach you one thing: it is important to find good friends and be interesting enough to keep them close. My roommate and the girls across the hall were close enough to build fast friendships. On a drive for dorm-life necessities, I lobbed a conversational softball that I believed I could knock out of the park. I asked the car what their parents called them as kids. They all chimed in with typical answers like "sweetie pie" and "sugar-plum." I proudly announced that my dad called me Jiggers. As planned, the joke landed and they roared with laughter. Not in my plan, they made the collective decision to call me Jiggers for the rest of the trip and into the weeks following. Before I knew it, everyone was calling me that and, honestly, I didn't hate it. It felt more comfortable and congruent than the boring old Jennifer and automatic Jenny, Jen and Jenna nicknames that inevitably followed.

My friendship with Rosina simmered slowly. I was busy becoming Jiggers and she was dating a cute boy. I assumed my first impression of her and her perfectly particular outfit and mannerisms meant that she was a little too buttoned up for me. Messy people were more my speed. It wasn't until an afternoon well into our second semester that we both ended up in the library near one another.

I was looking through a shelf of research journals and she had set herself up at a nearby table with books, notebooks and a two-liter soda bottle she had emptied and repurposed to hold her water. We shared a quick whispered greeting and I turned my back to her. I heard her reach for the bottle, unscrew the cap and tip the entire contents backward taking gulp after giant gulp until the bottle made a loud popping noise from suction. Then she tipped it back down with a slosh, and drew it from her mouth gasping for air. Deeply concerned, I turned to look at her. In a dramatic motion, she wiped her mouth with the arm of her sweatshirt and said, "*gasp....* Sorry.... *gasp...*I just really love water!"

That sloppy, gasping joke convinced me to sit with her

and we began the greatest best-friendship the world has ever known. On campus, people knew us only as a unit. If you saw me, you saw her and if you didn't see her, I knew where she was. We were Jiggs and Ro, a more notorious pair than peanut butter and jelly, than Tigger and Pooh. We ate every meal together, shared all our secrets and encouraged each other's dreams. I was the quiet and insecure one and she was the boisterous and confident one. We would sit for hours after meals as I watched her slay the Christian ministry boys in heated debates with her sword of Biblical knowledge. She would push me to talk when I was sad and read my moody little poems. I taught her the ways of being easy-breezy and she taught me how to stand up and speak out. Sing it if I have to! Nowhere was Rosina more of an enthusiastic cheerleader than when it came to me playing guitar.

Before college guitar had always been a private hobby. It was my thing. My very secret thing. My mom often retells stories of hearing me behind the closed bedroom door forming chords and plucking the strings one at a time until they all sounded clearly before unleashing a fury of strums in the same key. If I had known she was listening, I would have quietly died choking on my own embarrassment. I was never big on live performances.

As a four-year-old, I remember sitting in the back seat of the station wagon signing my heart to Hall and Oates *Maneater* anticipating my moment to belt out my best "ooo-biti-swa-ooo" only to be caught by my dad's eyes in the rear view mirror simultaneously smirking and sparkling at how precious he found me. I would see him and go immediately limp and mute like a puppet who had the hand pulled out of her butt.

I loved being in the chorus and loved it more that I was tall and got to stand in the very back row. I secretly dreamt of having a solo, but even in the privacy of my own room rocking my hairbrush microphone, I pretended to be Richie Sambora, never Jon Bon Jovi. Solos were no-goes.

Frankly, there were a lot of things working against me performing. First, I was tall. Most leading roles for girls are downstage of their male co-star. A tall girl upstages a growing boy. That both hurts their fragile egos and is not aesthetically pleasing. Secondly, I was an alto. If you don't know anything about music, let me just tell you, most songs are keyed for tenor male voices and soprano female voices. Anywhere that multiple people sing together, altos are singing the often excruciatingly boring one or two note harmonies supporting the sopranos. We rarely, if ever, get the lead. I learned this truth as an 8-year-old in the elementary school chorus and a lifetime of singing has proven it over and over again.

In the mid-to-late 90s, a girl with a guitar had a lot of role models. Jewel, Alanis Morissette, Wynonna, Melissa Etheridge, and Sarah McLachlan were all in their prime. Christian subculture, never far behind the mainstream, wouldn't be upstaged offering their own versions of these icons. As a sophomore in college, walking down the hall of the dorm, I heard a haunting, enchanted song so beautiful it froze me and stole my breath. A single voice filled every square inch of the hollow hallway, not a drum, not a piano, not a guitar backing. Just a naked, vulnerable alto scaling up and down a delicate intonation of joy and despair.

"Who is this?!" I demanded. My friend Kristy was doing homework at her desk.

"This is Jennifer Knapp," she replied. Her eyes widened as

she put two and two together. "Dude, *you* should get her stuff, you would absolutely love her! This is *definitely* up your alley."

As if on cue, the tender acapella erupted into drums and acoustic guitar, and I was obsessed. Near immediately, I bought her album. It was vividly clear that whatever was breaking my heart at eighteen was breaking hers too. That CD and each subsequent release played on constant rotation in my jambox. Her lyrics understood me.

These songs showed me how it felt to belong. Not the sad kind of belonging I had known before where you cut off and distort parts of yourself to fit in, but being yourself and finding a same-ness with others. She was cool and smart and beautiful, and her music expressed my every longing. I didn't necessarily have the confidence to be vocal with my thoughts, but she at least made it feel okay to think them and provided me with the opportunity to sing them out loud in the solitude of my dorm room.

It didn't occur to me to let anyone hear the music I was making because that felt arrogant, or narcissistic. It was so awkward to think about people having to be quiet and just listen to me drone on through verses, choruses, and bridges. And what if they hated it? Maybe I only sounded okay because the acoustics inside my head are just better than those outside and people listening might be exposed to something hideous and painful. Also, there were always people singing in church and school and...I mean...they weren't good. But everyone was always so nice to them. "Oh that was lovely," they would say. People lie. I don't need to be patronized.

It wasn't until spring semester of my sophomore year, after a lot of encouragement from Rosina, that I would finally try. Our school was very conservative. We couldn't have dances or parties because they were immoral. It was the late nineties though and coffee was a huge deal. Once a semester, the student activities committee hosted an event they called The Coffeehouse. They bought fancy coffee mixes, pulled some puffy furniture into the dining hall, lowered the lights and invited people who felt so led to perform coffeehouse style material. Some people read poetry, some dramatic monologues, but most everyone played an acoustic song on piano or guitar. I very reluctantly told Rosina I was thinking about it, and she erupted with her typical enthusiastic support. From her perspective I simply had to do it and she would not allow me to say no.

As the event approached, I decided, undecided, and second guessed my song choice roughly 800 times. I wanted something easy, but not basic. It had to be profound, but also could only use the G, C and D chords. By the time the night arrived, I had decided on a song by the popular Christian band Third Day called *Thief*. It was a song from the perspective of the man crucified next to Jesus and his eleventh-hour repentance and salvation. Perfect.

Friends who knew I was going to play looked at me with bulging eyes and silently clapped their hands in excitement while smiling an exaggerated smile. I, terribly unfamiliar with such attention, could only smile back with what I hoped was a similar expression but was probably more akin to the face a deer makes before getting hit by a truck.

When my turn came, I rose to my feet and made the long walk to the stage. Once I arrived in the spotlight, the microphones, speakers and wires conspired to tangle themselves in a dangerous web of humiliation. My guitar nudged the mic stand and it screamed a jarring boom across the room. "I'm so sorry," I whispered into the hot mic while my butt cheeks twisted around the stool looking for balance. Should I sit on it? Lean on it? A compromise, perhaps. One leg up, one down. My guitar slipped around wildly on my corduroy pants as I fished for the lyric sheet I had crumpled in my pocket. I smoothed it on the music stand. After a cleansing breath, I began.

My song filled the cafeteria as everything and everyone else fell silent. My voice was soft and timid. The microphones strained to amplify me. Tension built in the lyrics and my voice grew louder catching the reverb added by crafty sound engineers. I heard myself from the monitors in a way I never had. It invited me to listen, but I had to keep singing.

My eyes pinched tightly through the first verse and chorus. When they opened to look at the next verse's first lyric, I dared to glance at the crowd. Faceless silhouettes stood motionless in the darkness beyond the spotlight. So many pairs of eyes stalked my every move, ears scooping up every note. My inner voice encouraged me as I crossed the bridge and final verse. "You're almost there, you're almost done."

As the last note hung in the air, the entire audience broke loose with applause. Some even rose to their feet or wiped away tears. Two very popular boys marched up to the stage and gave me hugs. What a rush! I was shook! It was truly unbelievable. It was a thrill unlike any feeling I had ever had. Rosina was smug. She had been right to push.

I played at every coffeehouse after that night. I played Jewel, The Beatles, and Peter, Paul and Mary. I played silly songs and moving songs and deeply profound religious songs. I played for Bible studies, and even a couple actual coffeehouses in town. It was a healing elixir to my shaky self esteem.

My guitar and I were inseparable until the day the music died. It was late fall, and unseasonably warm. Longing to sit under a tree like they do in those college pamphlets, I ran to my car to grab my guitar. It bonked and hissed a horrible sound when I ran my fingers across the strings.

"What the heck?" I said to myself as I turned it in my hands inspecting it closely. When I spotted the problem I gasped and immediately ran to the dorm. Winded, with my guitar in hand, I asked a couple of guys in the lounge if they had seen Rosina. They hadn't, but asked if I was okay. I shoved the guitar toward them and showed them how heat had splintered the neck into two pieces. They shook their heads confirming that, indeed, you can't leave a guitar in a hot car, and it was probably trashed. I was sick. How could I ever tell my parents I made such a stupid mistake? I only had a work study job at the library, I couldn't afford to replace it. I was ruined.

People tried comforting me and encouraging me that I could save up or maybe someone could lend me theirs, but I remained depressed and inconsolable. For weeks I sulked around campus like Eeyore without his tail.

At a chapel service some weeks later, I sat slumped in my chair, still in my pajamas wearing a ball cap. The chaplain was droning on and on about something lame. Very abruptly he called out my name and pointed in my direction. Nervously I sat up and he ordered me on stage.

"Jiggers, it has been brought to our attention that you recently suffered tremendous loss."

Was this how he was going to tell me someone I loved was dead? My eyebrows furrowed in fear and confusion. He continued.

"It's hard to witness someone you care about suffering

through grief and so a few folks got together to try and offer you some comfort."

Squinting at the audience, I strained to understand what was happening. At first they seemed as confused as me but swiftly their confusion turned to joy and they motioned for me to turn around. Behind us stood the guys from the lounge holding a new guitar. They had felt so terrible for me that day, they collected money from people around campus. I held the beautiful instrument as tightly as my heart embraced their message: they weren't just humoring me, they liked it when I played.

Senior year at an Evangelical University means two things: graduations, and engagements. All across campus girls swooned over one another's shiny little diamonds, squealing and hugging each other's necks, bouncing up and down together. The anticipation of clutching a Bachelor's Degree with my naked left hand offered me no assurances of a safe and bright future. The whole "husband and kids" thing escaped me. But God is smart, therefore, he must have better, more important plans for me. I knew the answer before I even asked Him. I would make the biggest statement of devotion to God an evangelical human could possibly make. Obviously, I was supposed to travel the world and tell everyone about how much God loved them and everyone would clamor to the feet of Jesus and away from the horrible deceptive religions of their youth. Jesus could use me in powerful ways if I would only say, "Here am I, Lord, send me!" I was being called into missions!

Thumbing through my Bible, I saw reassurances of my new calling leaping off the pages. We shouldn't be living the way others live. We shouldn't be buying big houses and nice cars and investing in our 401k. Jesus told us that we needed to sell everything and give to the poor. Don't store up treasures on Earth! Certainty swelled in my chest. We needed to take up our cross and follow him. It was inconceivable that so many other Christians were just lining up for the rat race when we were the keepers of the Good News. God's love had hit me over the head like a 2x4. I wouldn't have been able to live with myself if I thought there were people in other countries dying without a saving knowledge of Christ. Their blood would be on my hands. How could I *not* be a missionary? How could anyone *not* be a missionary?

At the announcement of my plan, it was as though a spotlight swept from stage right and burned its heat down on my forehead. Invitations were made for me to speak and sing in Chapel services, and I was interviewed by the church district newspaper. Younger students would stop me in the commons to tell me I was inspiring and ask burning questions of how it felt to be called. People wanted to know details. What would I be doing? Was I afraid? How much money did I need to raise? They found me fascinating and exciting. Their expectant faces slowed my responses as the weight of my words felt heavier, holier. Tightly clutching cursory responses of utmost humility in my sweaty hands, I learned to deal them out with flare and precision of a Vegas blackjack dealer, hopefully masking the panic that seized in my chest. My popularity was blazing. No one even noticed my naked left ring finger.

Shuffling into the student center one day, there was a crowd milling around the front desk. Homecoming was approaching and everyone was nominating the court. Scribbling the names of all the best girls in school, I dared not dream of winning it myself. I allowed only an occasional fantasy of owning a tiara when I heard I was nominated. Weeks later, after several minutes of pinching the inner sleeve of my Dad's best suit between two nervous fingers, amid cheers of classmates, I exchanged Dad's elbow for the Kings and leaned down to accept a crown I never saw coming. It made no sense to me. It was the highest honor a 20 year old Evangelical college student can give to her classmate, and it was mine. I was the Homecoming Queen. I imagine many of those women shook a fist at my victory. They were prettier, Godlier, and more "proverbial" than me. Knowing this, I humbly accepted it and did my best to always display gratitude for the unmerited favor, to this day, pulling it out during games of two truths and a lie, because nobody ever believes that shit.

Still unsure of where the missionary board would send me, my daydreams would float to wild landscapes and exotic destinations. Haunted by the memories of nearly failing French in high school, I focused my meditations on English speaking countries. I knew there were places in Africa that spoke English. I could see real life lions, or elephants, or giraffes!

Maybe I would go to the Australian Outback and enchant aborigines with tales of Jesus by the light of a campfire. Perhaps I'd be in the orphanages of Romania leading sick orphans in Bible study. I could whisper the secret truth of Jesus from behind a hijab as I lived undercover amongst the Muslims of Uzbekistan. A tickle of self-awareness would scratch the back of my conscience: Jesus, fresh water, and childcare are good things we are bringing to these people, right? This isn't insulting, is it?

That's the tragic underbelly of being a Christian missionary, the only thing you need to be leveraged by the modern church is a raised hand. You don't have to understand the culture you are infiltrating, you don't have to be brought up to speed on the historical, ecclesiastical or political context, and you don't even really have to understand theology. You just have to be audacious enough to think God needs your voice to reach people.

One ordinary afternoon, I got the call. Misty from the main office in Indianapolis was on the phone to tell me where they wanted me to go. The board had decided they needed me to work in Split, Croatia. The recent war had left the country hurting and they needed more support for the work there.

"Awesome!" My voice cracked. They speak some weird hard language there. "What kind of work would I be doing? Rebuilding cities? Orphans?"

"Well, no..." Misty shared, "You'll be teaching English and taking people out for coffee. Building relationships. Just whatever the long term missionaries need you to do."

Teaching English? Interesting. I loved coffee, that was a no brainer. Building relationships, learning Croatian: scarier. My chest tightened and my fingers tingled. This gave me something concrete to envision. My anxiety drove me to the library.

According to my research, the country I would be serving was a Catholic nation. My Pap-Pap was Catholic and unlike other evangelicals, I hadn't yet decided the Catholics were lost and going to Hell. It was splitting hairs, but I was told that because Catholics reach out to a variety of sources for help (hear Mary and the saints), they aren't really counting on the grace of Jesus. Priests blocked their pathway to God. Confession and penance insured a person's salvation as a catholic, not atonement.

It appeared my big plan to go reach the unreached became more of a Martin Luther mission of reformation. It was much less glamorous than traipsing through the jungle, wrestling lions and telling others a story they had genuinely never heard. But it was necessary. Maybe there was someone in a predominantly Catholic nation who had never heard of Jesus. Anything was possible. I accepted and I went.

# 4

# Beginning

Probation doesn't exactly sing of confidence. Probation says, "we don't trust you can handle this and we'll be keeping our eyes on you for a bit." So I wasn't teeming with pride when I got accepted to grad school on academic probation. The program director let me know that my recent test results were acceptably average, but my GPA from college was just too low for traditional admission. All that prancing around getting homecoming queen meant I hadn't exactly applied myself. But, she explained, the combination of the years I had spent in the real world post college and some undetermined quality she felt from me inspired her to give me a chance. I just had to make A's to prove I was worth the risk. No pressure.

On the first day of class, I packed up my favorite pens, a fresh notebook and all the courage I could find. My admission to school was in the middle of the academic year so I was joining a cohort already in progress. They had 30 weeks of school under their belts and all the subsequent confidence. My first class with them was a basic skills class. This is the class that teaches you how to sit with someone and listen.

When I walked through the door on my first day I was shocked to see half a dozen bright and gleaming twenty somethings. Therapists were supposed to be old people, gray and wise. I don't know why it never occurred to me that those old wise people might have pursued their therapy degrees right out of undergrad. I picked the seat nearest the door, in case there was an emergent need to run for my life. I unpacked my notebook and pen and watched as my new young friends pulled out their laptops and began clickety clacking on their keyboards.

When the professor walked in, my embarrassment grew. She too was at least 8 years younger than me. I was only 35, did I look as geriatric as I felt? Those fifteen years had flown by, but apparently I could have been earning a PhD and becoming a full professor. Swallowing hard, I buried the thought that my life was already a waste.

Our first activity was a control test. She wanted us to just have an investigative conversation with the person next to us. Spend five minutes getting to know as much information as you can and be prepared to report on what you have learned. I listened first. My partner seemed sweet and quiet. She looked at the floor and picked at her thumbs as she spoke. She started out slowly, sharing her name and a few spare details. But by the first minute mark she was crying and spilling a very full can of worms on the floor between us. The subject was supposed to be "what did you do on winter break" and boy, did my partner have a tough one. By the end of her time her husband had left, the kids had run away, she had crashed the car, and her father had died. She was in a puddle, and I was doing my best to help her clean up the mess. When it was my turn to give my report of her details, I shared very little. I just placed a hand over my heart and let everyone know she had a rough break, but she sounded strong and brave to me. She looked at me with gratitude and the professor commented that it sounded like some real therapy had taken place in our group. I didn't know what she meant yet, but it did feel good to sit with her and shoulder this stuff together.

Starting something entirely new is always a wild mix of scary and exciting. On the one hand, you have no confidence and everything you attempt is awkward and bumpy. But on the other hand, no one expects you to be any good at it, so when you mess up you're met with compassion and giggles. My first six months in Croatia were a perfect illustration of the hot stew of feelings a new beginning can create.

My flight into Split landed well after sunset. The darkness on the drive home masked the city. To my travel weary eyes, what I could see under the glow of the occasional street light looked scary and foreign. Billboards along the road mocked me with their strange words. Buildings loomed over me, vanishing into the dark sky above. It was scary, sure, but my exhaustion had a bigger influence over me. By the time my roommates showed me to my new room, I could only collapse in gratitude and sleep.

When I woke the next day, bright sunshine had rinsed the peril from the landscape and tipped my emotional scales back toward excitement. From my window I could see a lush green mountain that sloped into a sparkling blue sea. Between my house and the mountain stood a massive soccer stadium and streets that bustled with traffic. The air was alive with honks and chattering pedestrians laughing in conversation.

My teammates took me for a walk down the road and into the narrow marble walls of Diocletian's Palace. Worn to a glaze by time and weather, the walls rose high around us, a testament of the advancements of ancient architecture. Roads were reduced to hallways, too narrow for cars. They hummed with people, exotic and beautiful, shopping for wares or chatting at bistro tables while sipping coffee. You could almost hear the rhythmic footsteps of distant Roman Soldiers marching to defend the King's interests.

Several times that day I had to remind myself that I was a missionary making a huge sacrifice for God. It came more naturally to think of myself as a jet setting world traveler being romanced by beautiful land and culture. But, there was work to be done in the country that tourism hid from casual observers.

Their unemployment rate was painfully high after the recent war. Jobs were difficult to come by. You couldn't be so much as a waitress without being fluent in English as tourism was the most profitable industry. Many residents carried their own personal trauma from the war itself. People showed signs of frayed emotions, hair-trigger anger and jumpy responses to loud noises. A brief trip inland revealed buildings scarred by mortar shells and warning signs of landmines yet unrecovered.

Croatians forged their lives around the chaos, skilled at adapting to pressures over which they had no control. They were captivating people. Enchanting and cultured to the visiting eye, but rich with hard won wisdom to anyone who offered to stay long enough to know them. My heart knew they didn't need me. They might even be better off without me.

It would have been nice to be able to say I held on to that flash of wisdom, but I was young and easily distracted by shiny things. Nothing shone as brightly as my teammates. They were an elite group of people. My insecurity and uncertainty mixed to make noxious fumes that left me feeling like an outsider among them. Taking my cues from them, I tried my best to lean into the experience and fully embrace the culture around me. I tasted every food and took a thousand horrible pictures. True to the paradoxical form of Eastern Europe at the time, life there was as invigorating as it was terribly exhausting.

Teaching English proved to be as much of a challenge as you might imagine. We only had translators present in class the first day to help everyone start on the same page logistically. Once students returned for the second week we were left to stare at one another uttering brief English phrases over and over as we mimed their meaning with exaggerated faces and body language. Eventually someone in the class would shout out a phrase in Croatian, translating for all the other students and they would nod and hum their collective understanding. As weeks turned into months our conversations grew somewhat covering foods we liked to eat, weather we enjoyed, and our favorite hobbies. I wouldn't have the opportunity to have real conversations with my students until the the Christmas party when I would be shocked to learn many of them were doctors, professors and judges. Subconsciously, their weak English skills had sabotaged my ability to see them as the deeply intelligent men and women they were. I suppose it's hard to flex your intellect when all you can say is "I like cheese."

Don't you worry, friend, the Lord kept me humble. Any arrogance I might have been tempted to gather from being the teacher was immediately resolved once I left the English classroom for the Croatian speaking streets of the real world. Ignorant human would have been a compliment compared to the actual assessment of my Croatian language skills. Once in a meeting, everyone agreed that I spoke Croatian like a monkey. The primate flavor of my language was somewhat alleviated when I abandoned pieced together vocabulary for full length memorized sentences. My first sentence,"Ja učim Hrvatski, to je sve što mogu reći, (I'm learning Croatian, this is all I can say)" was so articulate people would be inspired to ramble on for minutes at a time before I was able to slide in my second best sentence, "oprosti me, nisam ništa od toga razumjela (forgive me, I understood none of that)."

The simplest tasks became difficult, and robbed me of any breezy confidence I had earned back home. Buying a loaf of bread required dictionaries and patience. My only solace came from my little apartment where I lived with two other Americans. Such peace awaited me in that place. It warmly insulated me from the foreignness beyond our door. Comfort developed from the pattern I had created of teaching English classes by day and exploring the city in the evenings. It was easy to take risks when my little America awaited me every night.

My roommates were awesome. Our personalities gelled and we operated like a well oiled machine. We kept common areas clean and all chipped in. While doing chores, we often sang together in beautiful harmonies. We gave each other space to rest and breathe, but gently rescued one another from falling off a lonely ledge into isolation. We challenged each other with Bible verses and brought each other small thoughtful gifts. The peace of home helped make the stress of daily life more tolerable.

The apartment was nice, but my absolute favorite place in the whole city was on the stage at church playing on the worship team. I may have not known the words we were singing, but I knew music, and fitting into my place in the band felt as close to home as I had found. The local church had been gifted a Fender Jazz bass that no one had ever played. Reasoning that it can't be much different from guitar, I decided to take it home and learn to play it. For a while, my fingers throbbed from the fat strings and I barely graduated beyond holding up the bottom of the chords with a single note, but I felt very much at home behind the massive instrument. It fit my large frame proportionately and I loved hanging it low on my waist and thudding its strings with a careless cool.

Singing Croatian was also much easier than speaking it. At first I only sang a few phrases in back-up of the lead singers, but before long I was leading songs for prayer night or Bible studies. It helped my pronunciation, but not my vocabulary. Imagine only being able to communicate in worship music-speak. I didn't know how to say "I think I might have a fever." But I knew, "Open the eyes of my heart, lord."

By my six month anniversary, I could ask for a Coca-Cola, and a loaf of bread. I could buy a bus ticket and get to any part of the city by myself. My passion for cherry strudel, hot chocolate, and journaling sessions in cafes on the Adriatic waterfront had grown. It felt good. This was my new life. This was exactly the exciting, world changing significance I was born to have.

# 5

# Sexual Dysfunction

Graduate school was rife with opportunities to be honest. For the most part, telling the truth was tolerable. Sometimes, however, it was accompanied by nausea, trembles and a little voice screaming in the back of your mind, "don't do it." My first experience in higher education was at a very small, very Christian university. We rarely spoke of shameful things and if we did it was never in a co-ed crowd. My graduate school was a bigger, more secular, liberal arts university. No topic was off limits and participation was required.

We discussed nearly every angle of the human experience, and classes were structured to invite self-exploration and vulnerability. You didn't just write a paper on the effects of a client's family system, you explored your own family system in front of the class. You didn't just learn how to administer psychological evaluations, you had your neighbor administer them on you. There were classes about relationships, prejudice, conflict styles and your ego's shadow. My awkwardness peaked during a class called Sexual Dysfunction. In this course, we talked about all manner of embarrassing things like impotence, pornography, and sexual identity. The lecture that day was on the famous Kinsey scale.

According to Kinsey, not all people are completely straight or completely gay. More often, we fall on the spectrum somewhere between the two extremes. Scoring a zero on the scale meant you were exclusively heterosexual and had never had a homosexual thought or experience. Scoring a six meant you were exclusively homosexual without so much as a fleeting temptation to try anything hetero.

The professor radiated with a smug excitement as she introduced our class to the activity she had set up to help us grasp the concepts.

"I've taped signs to the floor of the hallway outside. To the left is zero, that's exclusively hetero." She pointed in the doorway like a flight attendant giving safety instructions. "The other end is six, that is exclusively homosexual thoughts and behaviors. The hall in between represents the spectrum from zero to six. We're gonna line up where we believe we each identify. *Be Honest* everyone, there is no shame in your place on the scale."

I had been choking back some level of anxiety throughout the lesson, but the activity really made my heart race. I wondered if this was really necessary. "What a flagrant display of deeply personal information," I thought as classmates shuffled around me. "Who in their right mind admits to homosexual thoughts? And in mixed company?" I looked at my classmates and saw some others had blushed cheeks and were giggling awkwardly as they took their place.

Two guys raced each other to the straight end and put their backs against the wall to illustrate they couldn't possibly be straighter. A chuckle over their insecurity bubbled from my gut despite having felt the exact same insecurity. Their overcorrection struck me as a challenge. The truth was flirting with me, but she and I had never been seen in public together this way before.

"Well this is embarrassing." muttered my friend Charlotte. Charlotte was my hilarious, albeit mildly embittered, lesbian friend. We had been sitting next to each other throughout this particular class and I really enjoyed her sidebar color commentary. Incidentally, she was the only "professional lesbian" I had ever considered a good friend.

In my very limited experience with lesbians, I had maybe known four of what I would call "professionals." Strictly speaking the only real requirement of being considered a professional lesbian was to just be out and pursuing relationships with women or in a relationship with a woman. Anecdotally, they also wore cargo pants, had multiple tattoos, used carabiners, and drove Subarus. If my anxiety were adding her opinion, they'd also be scary, masculine, needy and make me feel uncomfortable. But that really only described the one or two women I had met in college that I knew were gay and frankly, they were all of those things. The truth is, professional lesbians made me uncomfortable because they were honest, knew what they wanted, and that was intimidating. Charlotte was not intimidating, nor did she make me feel uncomfortable. She was like me in most respects.

"You okay, man?" I had to ask. Charlotte seemed stressed.

"Yeah, I think I'm just the only gay person here, so this will just turn into "Everyone! Look at Charlotte way down at the end all by herself! A real lesbian in the wild!""

I laughed with her. "That sucks."

"Where are you gonna stand?" Her question lilted with a hopefulness that I would join her.

"I dunno yet. I'm processing. But good luck."

She darted her eyes at me playfully curious, but only nodded as she turned and took her inevitable position as the lone perfect six. My reluctance glued my feet to the floor. My position was more complicated than hers. Depending on who asked, I "technically"could still label myself a virgin. I had successfully resisted sleeping with every man I had ever dated.

In other circles, I was most definitely *not* a virgin. Words like slutty, insatiable, seductress would have been more fitting. Pressed onto those memories with sticky adhesive were labels reading "Bad Detour" or "Moral Failing." They were indicative of my flawed character, not my sexual identity.

Negotiating with the hissing whispers of those mistakes, I took my place with two other people standing near the three. I turned back and looked at Charlotte, knowing I might technically belong there with her. She smiled and raised an eyebrow and my embarrassment set my skin on fire.

# 6

# The Boys

A waitress flipped a little square napkin on the table in front of me, and set a foggy bottle of beer on top. Charlotte sat across from me, tipping her bottle back but carefully holding eye contact while drinking.

"Sooo, a three?' she asked. "I'm all ears."

A laugh puffed from my nose and I took a long drink to stall. We are aspiring therapists, nosey by nature. I knew I wasn't going to get away with dropping any juicy clues without a thorough follow up investigation.

"I mean," I said, still stalling, "I've just had more than incidental sexual thoughts and behaviors with both sexes, I'm just trying to be honest."

"Uh-huh, okay, so you're dating a dude right now, yes?"

"Yeah, for a while. But we haven't slept together yet." I hung the word yet on the end of my sentence as a smokescreen to convince her that sleeping together was even something he and I had talked about or something I wanted.

"Really? Wow. You've been dating like a year now though, right? What are you waiting for?"

She watched my face as I considered my answer and then beat me to it.

"Oh, you're waiting for marriage," she said. "Have you slept with any dude?"

As an adolescent in the church, you are taught, in no uncertain terms, that sex is bad for single people. Spending time with people of the opposite sex is the muddy edge of a slippery slope that leads to teen pregnancy and absolute destitution. Refraining from sex, sexual activity, sexual immorality, making out, kissing or even dating was the agreed upon position for all good young churchgoers in the 90s. We wore purity rings to display our virginity, we hung out in big groups, we kissed dating goodbye, shamed the sluts, and stayed up late night dreaming about how great waiting would make our wedding night.

We didn't just avoid sex, we avoided even the appearance of impropriety. Doors stayed open, feet on the floor, and men and women were never alone together. Sexual desires were ravenous beasts that would devour us if we stopped worrying about them for even a moment. I naively believed everyone was telling the truth, but after being out of college for a couple decades I can now confirm that there were probably only a handful of us who could hang our bachelor's degrees next to our shiny unblemished virginity.

Maybe it would help Charlotte understand if we toured the halls of the men I had dated. My first boyfriend was Jack. We were 17. I had decided it was time to try dating and being that he was respectable and said he was a Christian, I figured he was good enough. We went to church together and occasionally we would go out. He even took me to the senior prom. He treated me so well, presenting me with compliments, candy, and mix tapes of country music ballads. When I called to break up with him, he hadn't done anything wrong. It wasn't him, it was me.

Jack was my first and longest relationship, the grand marshal to a sad parade of failed attempts at intimacy with men. Any man that followed had to stand in his shadow and most would fail miserably.

James was dark, and a bit strange. He wore capes and played with swords. He also either wore eyeliner, or needed several more hours of sleep per night. He was very funny and thought I was pretty adorable, so we went out once. To our first date he wore a long black trench coat and black gambler hat. He was skilled at bringing much of our conversation back around to his favorite subject: spiders. We had no physical contact. We stayed friends briefly, then he faded back into the shadows.

Ron was tall. Very tall. At nearly seven feet, he had to duck under door frames. Always elusive about what kind of job he had, I felt sure it wasn't lucrative when he pulled up in a Dodge Neon. There was nothing wrong with his car, but it was so small I felt a secondary embarrassment at watching him pry his seven foot frame out of it, and then fold himself back up again when it came time to leave. The first time I witnessed this spectacle, Ron had come to pick me up for our first date. He took it upon himself to bend down and slather a very drippy open mouthed kiss on me. Afterward, he smiled proudly and said, "I know, right?" I was not as impressed as I, apparently, should have been.

Andy had social anxiety. I met him online and never actually met him for a date because he was afraid of public spaces. We texted for several weeks attempting to get to know each other in a way that didn't frighten him. He was a devoted Christian, staunch republican, and passionately pro-life. He peppered me with questions looking for me to blow just the right dog whistles. How did I feel about the Jews? Is abortion murder? Was I pre-millennial or post? Did I own a gun? Did I support his right to own a gun? Who did I vote for in the last election? I scraped up my best responses and he invited me over to his house. I suppose that meant I passed, but a date with a stranger in his home was no prize.

Rich was cute. He was tall and had dimples and big blue eyes. We met for some fast food and laughed and talked about a lot of shared interests. We had a great time until the end of the date when Rich showed me that our food wasn't as fast as his hands. I halted his advances so firmly I scared myself a little. Had he taken my brake check like a man and not a petulant child, we might have gone out again. Alas, he made his choice and I made mine.

Russ was sweet and kind and had a beautiful smile. At times he could be a bit awkward, but I found it endearing. He was also a wildly creative artist and it was really impressive to watch him work his magic. He was in his early 30s and still a virgin for religious reasons. I thought the choice was noble and felt a deep relief at knowing it wouldn't come up. We dated for months before having to sadly acknowledge that neither of us felt a sparkle. If I had thought for a moment that I could build a happy life without heat, it would have been with him. But he deserved passion as much as me. It does my heart good to know he finally met that dream girl and now both of their eyes sparkle at their adorable son.

There were others. Affairs too brief to remember their names. They lavished me with lengthy text messages like "W Y D?" to woo me into rapture. They tried tantalizing me with blurry pictures of their penises laid artfully against the backdrop of their dirty bathroom floors. They attempted to impress me with conversational prowess by telling me their day was "fine."

"And that's it, I never slept with any of them."

"Wow, I'm so glad I'm a lesbian," she sighed. "I mean, I've dated my share of winners, but that list just sounds depressing."

Depressing doesn't begin to describe it. When I'm telling the stories back to back I can spin it all into comedy gold and have people laughing with me over my misfortune. But living through both the experiences and the long lonely chapters between them was troubling. I could only conclude from the data that there was either something wrong with all men, or my picker was malfunctioning.

It took only a brief silence for Charlotte to ask the question that truly interested her. "How about girls? Have you tried dating a girl?"

# 7

# Her

Laci was a Californian. She wore her flip-flops and sunglasses like culture, a style I had only poorly appropriated from surfing magazines. Her cheeks were freckled tan and her hair fell obediently into whatever style she carelessly requested. Eight months had passed since I had moved to Croatia and she was the latest edition to the ministry team. It was my responsibility to help her get settled.

It was serious business to mentor her. We spent hours together learning about bus tickets, and money exchange. I taught her a few phrases and introduced her to the best cafes and restaurants. We built a strong connection quickly. It was encouraging to contrast her ignorance with my experience. She needed me and I needed that. Her confidence in me felt safe and empowered me to try new things.

Her tenacity had her outpacing my skill set by leaps and bounds. Once she didn't need my help getting around we were forced to manufacture reasons to spend time together. We'd go for long walks, and sit for hours staring at the sea sharing our deepest selves. She was talented at focusing the conversation on me and offering observations that were encouraging and uplifting. She breathed fresh air into my experience and inspired me to consider extending my contract from one year to two.

She smiled with such pride when I broke the news.

"Dude, are you for reals? I'm so stoked to hear that!" she bounced up and down on her bed. "Next year is going to be so rad! The youth ministry can take off, we can busk with worship music in the streets. We are gonna have the best time!"

Joy poured out of me with laughter. Her excitement tickled me. "I love how happy you are to hear this!" I told her.

Her roar faded to a hush. "Dude, you know what we should really do?" .

"What?" I leaned toward her.

"We should live with Croatians!"

The giant goofy smile I held while listening melted from my face to make room for mouth gaping disbelief as I processed her statement.

"Huh?" I uttered.

"Yeah girl! Think about it! My friend said most missionaries live with nationals so that they can learn language and really experience culture. It would totally rock!"

My gut reaction was, "Yikes," and "Heck No!" Not having a sanctuary in which to hide was against everything I loved about life. This did not seem possible. If my heart had spoken it would have said I was completely against it. There was no way that would ever work for me. It was hard enough to live with other Americans and, if you asked me, I was plenty submerged into Croatian culture.

Being a good roommate and not bothering anyone, for any reason, ever, required skill, and effort, not to mention language! How would a Croatian tell me I was a bother? What if I made them mad? Or worse, what if I broke something? My mind paced in deep concern. I pressed hard against the strained dam walls holding back all my worst thoughts. This whole experience had already been so scary and lonely. What the hell was I going to do without my precious American apartment cocoon?

Remembering Laci was staring at me, I clasped a figurative hand over the mouth of my quaking inner critic. My buddy is just standing there, heart in her hands, waiting for me to affirm her excitement. Was I going to let her down? I smiled at her.

"You're insane, Lace. Let's do it!"

The local apartment I moved into was a moderate size. My bedroom was large, with room for a bed, couch and television. My roommate, who was a few years my senior, spoke very little English. Her little white dog spoke often, though it was unclear what language he was using. I stayed in my room. She probably thought I hated her, but the truth is I was terrified all the time. The language barrier was harder than I had imagined. I couldn't ask for anything I needed or understand anything she needed from me. My only choice was to languish in quiet despair. I did some of my finest languishing in that apartment.

Laci had the opposite problem. She lived with Nana, the sturdy mother of church friends who had lived alone before my friend arrived. After moving in, Laci became Nana's new granddaughter. Laci was so tightly secured under Nana's wing that she had trouble getting out of the house most of the time. She was a mess, unable to think or navigate life freely without having to consider her new grandmother's opinions. Their ideas nearly always conflicted. The passion of the Californian freethinker didn't jibe well with the wisdom of old-world Eastern Europe.

Thoughts of Laci crowded out my suffering. My heart lifted at the comforting "warp zuppa dorp" of the radio interference that preceded the arrival of her texts. She was always ready with a "Miss you" or a "Where you at?" or "This creep on the bus is lookin at me funny." She was one of only a few rays of light in a dark time. She was such a courageous girl.

On rare, mystical evenings, it would get late, and her exhaustion would allow a peek behind her brave facade. God, I loved those times. Sitting in the near darkness, watching tears cascade down her freckled cheeks, she longed for home, for rest. The pain in her eyes renewed my sanity. If she hurt, it was because it was painful, not because she (or I) was weak. Her suffering broke my heart, but her tears watered an oasis for my own pain. Commiserating would happen more and more often and last longer each time. Words became less and less necessary. Sometimes we just held each other, collecting tears.

Our friendship gave people something to talk about. The long-term missionaries talked. The short-term missionaries talked. Croatians talked. They talked to me, to her, to each other. The gossip surrounded us like swarming yellow jackets. They didn't approve of our increasing time together. They tossed around words like inappropriate, co-dependent, and needy. Their labels flared my defiance and only made me want to meet with her more.

We weren't isolated from everyone in the confines of our relationship. We were close with the other guys on the team. One evening, they extended an invitation to come over to their house and sample local beer. I was reluctant, but Laci was all in. It was the definition of scandalous. The last time I had a whole Zima my best friend cried for two days about slippery slopes. Not wanting to be a party pooper, I agreed to join in.

We spent several hours with our friends, laughing and sharing six beers and a bottle of something I couldn't identify but burned my mouth with the same ferocity as the brown mouthwash I always had to use at Grandma's house. Laci giggled and tossed them back with a reckless twinkle in her eye. I watched her with a smile and a shake of my head.

As the evening progressed, she grew less inhibited. It might have been the alcohol, or she might have been high on the fumes of rebellion in the air. She was faking it if you ask me. It gave off the same vibes as "A Very Special Episode of *Saved by the Bell.*" There was no way her behavior was real, or that Mark-Paul Gosselaar nailed a scene this accurately. Still, I didn't want her going home to Nana smelling of alcohol and risk us all getting in trouble for it. I wrangled her into my apartment. She threw up once and I helped her brush her teeth and put her to rest in my bed. She patted the mattress beside her insisting I didn't sleep on the couch. I obliged.

My dreams were fast-paced and strange. I was an alcoholic now; this was to be expected. Tortured by the content of a nightmare, I roused myself to consciousness. In the blur between awake and asleep I discovered that Laci was touching me. I swatted her hand and twisted her arm by the wrist both to wake her and to lead her to her feet, out of my bed.

"Dude, what are you doing?!" I shouted with a hushed voice so I didn't wake anyone. She stood in the middle of the room confused, ashamed.

"I don't know, I was asleep. I don't know. I'm so sorry!"

"Do you think I wanted you to do that? Do you think I'm

some kind of nutbag? Are you? What is wrong with you? What possessed you to think that was okay? Are you like a frikken lesbian?" I growled at her. I was appalled that she had done it, hurt that she thought I would want it, and terrified by how much I liked it.

"I told you I was sorry, please stop, I'm sorry." She was crying harder now. She reached for excuses: disorientation, confusion, bad dreams, alcohol, but I continued to seethe.

"I think I should just leave," she whimpered, "It's only a few miles home, I'll just walk."

Her threat to leave broke my angry trance. It was 2am. That was stupid.

"No, Laci, that's dangerous. Don't be ridiculous." She couldn't leave. Safety. Ministry. Nana. Darkness. Alcohol Breath. Seeing her tears falling reminded me that I was normally the one who caught them. These drops were for me, because of me, because I yelled.

She raced around the room to look for her things, stumbling, trembling. I envisioned what might happen if she left. The guilt and shame she would feel might come between us. I might lose her. I needed her. With my most earnest voice I pleaded with her.

"Lace, seriously, I don't want you to go. I want you to stay. I'm fine. I'm sorry I yelled. I was just really surprised."

She turned to look in my eyes and check for sincerity. It was there, so she relented. She dropped her things and sat down on the couch, stating she would sleep there only until the buses were running. My fear wanted more. I wanted closure, I wanted to reconnect to my friend, my partner in crime.

My heart rate was completely back to normal, and the fog of

anger had evaporated. I sighed loudly. I insisted she stop being weird and just come back to bed. I forgave her. An exaggerated smile sprang to my face to demonstrate that I was fine. I patted the bed like she had a few hours earlier and she reluctantly joined me.

Lying next to each other flat on our backs, hands above the blanket, and staring at the ceiling in the darkness, I tested our friendship with a tentative joke. She chuckled softly in reply, offering me a sip of relief. She admitted she was glad I let her stay but was afraid I was going to think she was weird now. With a heavy sigh through my nose, I turned toward her and propped up on my elbow to make eye contact. I reassured her that we were the same as we had ever been and it was going to take a lot more than this to change anything. Then I kissed her on her cheek, and she tearfully nodded her acceptance. Sensing my message hadn't gotten all the way through I playfully kissed her face again. Then again. Then again.

"Okay! Okay! I believe you!" she insisted, laughing in her full voice for the first time.

"No ma'am," I said, kissing her face again, playfully. "You gotta know we are just fine!" I kissed and kissed, and she chuckled delightfully. As I persisted in my silliness, her laughter faded to a giggle and then to a smirk. I paused my barrage, and she moved her face to the left slightly to signal her search for my eye contact. My smile melted as I met an unfamiliar, penetrating stare.

"Kiss my face again and I'll kiss you for real."

The air was sucked out of the room. Searching her face for answers, I found none. Her eyes were firm and fixed. Her eyebrows were raised slightly to match the dare she just handed me. Her lips looked new. Did I want them? Would I recover from what they did to me? What did this all mean about me? My mind wanted more time to contemplate the options, but my body already knew. Leaning forward slowly, leaving plenty of opportunity to stop me, I pressed my lips against her forehead, squarely between her eyes.

All my years of being gifted at abstinence fell crashing to the floor. This was the wild animal of temptation. Her kiss hit me with the fury of a hurricane. Everything inside of me sprang to life in rich colors. Every part of my body worked in perfect orchestration, instinctually, automatically. The urges swirling around inside me shook me and scared me and thrilled me. I desperately wanted every inch of her, and I wanted to give her every inch of me. Fuck!

# 8

# Liar

There comes a time in every therapist's life when she realizes that she too needs a therapist. I convinced myself that it was a matter of fully understanding my client's experiences in being vulnerable with a stranger, but really, I was longing to straighten out the mess in my own mind. Laci was not just an incidental homosexual contact. I loved her deeply for an extended period of time. In some ways, I even loved her still. Kissing her and falling off a lusty cliff of sexual desire wasn't the whole story. She wasn't even the only story. There was more to discuss.

Brandi had come into our sexual dysfunction class to talk about the psychological effects of sustained pornography use. Her short gray hair framed her clean and natural face. Thick rimmed glasses perched atop her nose to highlight her piercing gaze. Her clothes spoke a subtle androgyny and her shoes were comfortable. Her compassionate covering of a topic as difficult as pornography use coupled with her apparent gayness demonstrated that she would likely be a safe person to give my darkest secrets.

The leather couch squeaked beneath my thighs as I sat nervously across from my new therapist. A fuzzy little dog sniffed my sneakers as he walked by me, rejecting my bids for affection. Brandi smiled warmly at me and asked me how I felt school was going. Unsure if this was the actual therapy, I tried to answer wisely. She accepted with a nostalgic smile and probed for the reason I was seeking her help. By the time the session had reached the quarter hour, I was knee deep in the story of Laci.

On the one hand, there was love. Fresh and new and glorious. All those months building a foundation of caring for each other and, in many ways, it felt like it blossomed into a whole new wonderful thing. But I was wrapped up in peaking as an Evangelical missionary. This was a terrifying thing to uncover. I wish there were nothing more to it than being young and in love. It would have been so nice to experience all these new and exhilarating feelings without the baggage of having to integrate 'hopeless pervert' into my identity.

That's what the church would now label me. This wasn't your run-of-the-mill fornication found at the bottom of the slippery slope that moves every young couple to tears of repentance at the altars of summer camp. This was one of the sins that came with a death sentence. It was a terrifying thing to uncover about myself. That shit was bad. It was like I had been digging for treasure and uncovered a dead body. I didn't want to have to tell anyone what I had found. I was wrong. I was bad. I was broken. I was terrified. My body and heart didn't work as they were supposed to. It was all backwards. I was the worst possible thing.

I lied hard. I wanted her so much that I said whatever I or anyone else needed to hear but my true self was hungry for an honest conversation. On the one hand, I wanted someone to revel in my joy with me and ask for the saucy details. On the other, I wanted to confess, to have someone set me back on the path, and put all this foolishness behind me. But I could only talk to her about it, and I didn't want to for fear that she would get spooked, and I would never get to touch her again. God, I loved touching her. Her skin was so silky and warm. My every sense could draw up vivid memories of just her skin at any moment, drugging me into a drooling, staring, stupor. Goddamn this.

Journaling normally helped drain the confusion from my mind, but the risk of someone finding it was too great, so I could only fill my notebooks with passionate prayers to be rescued from mysterious selfish desires. She was so nice and beautiful and soft and warm. When I closed my eyes, I saw visions of us wrapped tightly in each other, delighted. Hands sliding across bodies, breath and heartbeats syncing while the reality of our lives evaporated into an inconsequential mist. When I opened my Bible, I saw condemnation, judgment, and eternal abandonment. Deceptive, and probably queer, I was deeply ashamed of both.

After a few months of our best pleading, we were allowed to move out of our nightmarish living situations and into a shared space. Conveniently, our rooms were connected by a balcony so that even after roommates moved in, we could sneak into each other's bed at night and find a set of waiting arms. Most mornings we woke twice. Once, tiptoeing into the other's room and reaching with our whole body to find the other waiting under the covers. After a few minutes spent basking in the sounds of quiet morning groans and hushed kisses, we'd retreat to our corners and stagger our good mornings from our respective bedroom doors.

Guilt and the power of our shared faith ebbed in countering cycles. Sometimes in the middle of the night while holding each other, one would start to cry with guilt and have to escape. We were never safe in our love from the judgment our faith had waiting for us. We were programmed to stick to the narrow path. That path didn't include loving each other the way we were.

"Couldn't you just stay this way forever?" she whispered. It was early morning and she had snuck into my room for a secret snuggle. Her mouth was close to my ear and made her words linger with a wet heat.

"Yeah," I said, "It's like the most comfortable place in all of time and space."

The long sheer curtain swelled and collapsed from the gentle cold breeze as I pulled her closer revealing new patches of warmth in which to bury ourselves.

"Tell me again about the house we're going to buy together."

"Oh yes, well," I said, painting a picture with my hand in the air, "We will live in a beautiful loft in downtown Nashville. It will have old brick walls and the ceilings will be twelve feet high. It will be above a coffee shop in a bustling part of town. We'll know the owner, Paul, who loves kayaking as much as he loves coffee. He lives across town with his dog Ulysses."

"And what will we be doing?"

"Of course, I will be a musician. After a couple years of playing in a local church band and singing in open mic nights, I'll get discovered and be a full-time songwriter for a record label. I'll have to write country music, but it's a living."

"And me? What will I do?"

"You? Hmm, you have actually taken a surprise route and are

a writer. You broke into young adult nonfiction with a book about bullying."

"What?! No no. I don't like that, pick something else."

"Oh okay, you…umm…okay…You are a famous dog trainer."

"Dog trainer?! How are you a musician and I'm a dog trainer?" she laughed.

"Well what do you want to be? You tell me!"

"I want to be the head of a big ministry, helping other people and changing the world," she cheered with a fist pumping in the air.

"Oh, of course," I said, the cold water of reality still dripping from my face. Inspired by the desire to hurt myself just a little more I asked, "What happened to us?"

"We figured it out," she said with a casual lilt. "We learned how to quit this part and were closer, better friends than ever." That's right. That's the plan. No future bed would know our bodies. No future room would hold our secrets. This was all temporary.

As hotly as I could love her in one moment, I could turn cold with sisterly love the next. I was supposed to be pushing her toward God, not wooing her away from him. No thought could rest on its own power uninterrupted for very long. I'd kiss her and my thoughts would scream, "You're going to Hell for this!" Or I would rest a hand on her shoulder in prayer and fight to not slide it down to the small of her back.

Occasionally, she would get all dolled up and I wouldn't be able to resist commenting.

"Wow, you look really good in that outfit," I'd say, head tilting to catch every angle.

"Hey! Cut that out!" She'd snap. "We are doing well right now! Don't mess it up!"

Other times, I would think I had a handle on the whole situation and arrive home only to be tossed against the wall in a lusty confrontation. Every instinct I had felt wrong no matter which part of me was driving. My old strategy of people-pleasing was failing me as neither of us could put a finger on which part of us deserved pleasure.

Everything we did was steeped in ambiguity. We found new and creative ways of making connections that still permitted us to have plausible deniability if people got suspicious. We planned vacations, organized group activities, and created ministry events. Time spent with one another could conveniently be labeled as either in a ministry activity or rigorously planning one. The ambiguity we hid ourselves in turned into more of a poison than a cover. We were so good at masking for others, I couldn't remember my own face.

Though it was steeped so thoroughly in the confusing mire of sin, I know she loved me as much as I loved her. That love was the stable core that kept us connected, though we were often tossed about by how we ought to express it. The most loving thing that Laci did for me during our brief affair happened on a single sunny afternoon after church. We were sitting at a cafe as she passionately argued with my inner critic.

"Give me one good reason why you shouldn't do it!" she demanded.

"I don't know, it just seems scary, I guess. Like...uggh. I don't know if I *can* do it."

"Ohmigod, Jeni," she fell backward in the booth in an exasperated lump, "You absolutely have to do it. This is it! This is your dream! Is it not?"

"Yeah, honestly, it is. But...seriously...you think it'll be good enough?"

She laughed quietly, rolled her eyes and looked at me with a face that told me I already knew her answer. "Jeni," she whispered, "Go be a rockstar!"

A friend told me of a guy he knew who owned a recording studio. He said he could set it up for us to come and record a few Croatian worship songs and make a CD for the church. Laci knew immediately that I should say yes, but it was intimidating. I'd never been recorded before and it was in a language I wasn't certain I spoke well. It was scary, but she believed in me, so I accepted.

When the day came, she followed me around like paparazzi with a camera dangling around her neck. She beamed with pride watching me sing through the control room window and met my anxious sighs with encouraging touches. It turned out to be kind of a hit. The Croatians in our church had never had Christian music in their language in their own homes before. Everyone loved it so much and I supposed I had grown in my language skills enough that no one said I sounded like a monkey. In fact, they reported, I even had just a hint of a Dalmatian accent.

Our last kiss was in a hotel in Germany. She had escorted me there to catch my flight back to the States. Two huge bags bulged off the sides of the hotel luggage trolley. The room was dark and she had just finished helping me run through my mental checklist ensuring I had everything I needed. We had been on the friendship side of our relationship for a while and I wanted to kiss her goodbye but I was hesitant to want it. It would be so poetic to have a last kiss in Europe before I left. Then whatever relationship we continued in the States could be pure holy friendship and the whole "lesbian" thing would just be a European fever dream. As I stared at her, wrestling within myself she gave in and pulled my face toward hers. The kiss was tender and sad. My lips clung to hers soaking in the year of beautiful desire, straining to never forget the taste of her. Tears pooled in my eyes and fell on her back as we hugged.

My flight was an overnight voyage across the ocean. Watching the tiny digital plane chart its path across the screen in front of me, my despair of leaving Laci faded into pure excitement at the thought of seeing family and friends.

"Welcome home!" cheered a small tribe of loved ones from the baggage claim of my local airport. Mom was holding a balloon and Rosina a little sign. They looked as ragged and tired as I felt. My connecting flight had been delayed by hours. What was supposed to have been a happy afternoon party, had become a late night sigh of relief. The people left standing when I finally arrived were a brave few with the flexibility to wait. They showed me pictures of the larger crowd having dinner together and I was touched that so many people came to see me return, but relieved they had not stayed.

Their hugs felt good, but I felt very different. I wondered if they could sense the changes, or if they wrote it off as culture shock. When you spend a long period of time in another culture you can become very disoriented. Even the most patriotic person can adopt the rhythms and ideologies of other cultures, and nothing shines a light on those changes quite like coming home again. It's just as much a culture shock to return as it was to move away.

Standing in a grocery store a few days after my arrival, the empty shopping basket hanging from my elbow, I stared at the refrigerated shelf, bewildered. I read each label carefully.

"Strawberry with real fruit, strawberry low calorie, strawberry greek non fat, strawberry greek full fat."

I could feel the tears in my eyes starting to build. *I just want yogurt!* What was once a simple Croatian choice between strawberry or plain was now a thirty-two square foot smorgasbord of hundreds of slightly variant cultured milk products. Just a few weeks ago my television programming choices were limited to Friends or Passions and suddenly I had 300 different channels with a new show playing every half hour.

I was cold to the bone regardless of where I went. Does it have to be seventy degrees everywhere? I went from walking 15,000 steps a day to less than 2,000. And everywhere I went, they were playing the same stupid song by some girl named Kelly Clarkson. They kept calling her an "Idol." America had a sickness.

I tried exploring all of these feelings with Laci when we could have time to connect. I would text or email her with all my wild observations and she met me with a compassionate knowing and soothed me with visions of us being able to someday live together again.

Her behavior changed as days passed. Her welcoming plans faded into a reluctance to dream with me. My invitations to connect were met with hems and haws of "we'll see" and "that's something to think about." Soon the time difference and physical distance were just too much to overcome.

I had only been gone a few weeks when she leveled me with a shocking revelation.

"I told our roommate about us," she admitted.

"What? You did? When?"

"We were just talking one night and it was late. You know how it goes, you just start talking and sharing, next thing I knew the cat was out of the bag and I was crying all over myself."

My silence was deafening, words weren't showing up for me. This was a huge blow.

"Omygosh, Jenni, you have to say something!"

"What did she say?"

"Actually, she was so nice. She said she didn't judge me, and she appreciated me telling her. It actually felt like such a relief. Someone knew and they didn't hate me."

"Well that's great," I snarked.

"You're mad."

"I'm not mad. I'm just freaked out. It's just a lot, you know? This was as much my secret as it was yours and you just made a decision without even asking me. I'm just like…I don't know… shocked!"

"You're right. I shouldn't have told her without asking. That's why I called. I want to tell the leadership team what happened. I think it's the right thing to do. But I don't want to do that without talking to you."

"What?! Laci, they're gonna kick you out! This isn't just some silly lie you told. They aren't going to understand."

"Jenni, if I don't belong here, then I don't want to be here. I want this off my chest. I have to do it."

"So you aren't really asking for permission, you're just telling me how it is. Thanks."

"Nope. If you tell me you don't want me to then I won't. But, personally, I would like to be free of this guilt."

The part of me that had built my whole world on my faith couldn't stand to hear that there would be people armed with this information and likely to judge me and label me something as offensive to me as "gay." It was excruciating to imagine the gossip that would ensue. Knowing how people had talked about lesbians with me guaranteed I knew what they would say about me. My name could not be associated with such ideas.

I wanted to stop her. I wanted to threaten her. But her chosen path was going to free her from any blackmail I could scrape together. Besides, I loved her. The turmoil we lived in for so long was heavy and difficult. She was not made for this much deception. She wasn't a "brush it under the rug" kind of person. It would be a horrible punishment to ask her to carry such a burden.

A part of me knew it was a righteous idea to come clean no matter how difficult it would be. That part of me was too anemic to walk into such blatant humiliation unassisted, but alive enough to admire her courage. The combination of my guilt, her longing for integrity, and my desire to make her happy was just enough to convince me to relent and allow her to make the confession she desired. Within a few hours of releasing her, she had a meeting time set.

A few days later, as I lay face down on the cheap carpet of my apartment in the dark hours of the morning scribbling prayers of protection and begging God to soften the hearts of those listening, Laci sat on a hard chair a half a world away and spilled my darkest secrets. Reports say that they were loving but swift in removing her from the team and sending her home. She would have to tell her supporters she was returning. She would need to tell her own pastor what had happened and seek absolution from him. The most important stipulation of all: she could never talk to me again.

She called me one last time to tearfully tell me the terms of her situation and apologize for all the ways she knew it would hurt me. She was right. It hurt me. It didn't make sense. Why couldn't we even be friends? Surely this was temporary. I convinced myself that it was hyperbole. Did they literally say we couldn't ever speak again? Perhaps we just stop talking until we were out of the spotlight. I stared at a bumpy speck of paint on the wall as I squeezed the rubber phone cord around my finger. The future was too painful to even attempt to imagine. All of my will focused itself on getting through that phone call. We could work things out privately later. I convinced myself that she would be back, cultivating just enough arrogance to say, "No worries, Laci, I love you. You go take care of yourself."

We hung up the phone, and true to the agreements she made with those to whom she confessed, she never spoke to me again.

# 9

# Help

Little snores pulsed rhythmically from the dog snuggling my thigh as I twirled a single curl of fur around my finger. Cooper, the therapy dog, had diagnosed me with anxiety and was performing his go-to intervention to soothe me. Therapy was difficult, but had become a pleasant space to process old stories.

In session, I was allowed to consider the light in my relationship with Laci. In that room it was possible that it was just young and innocent love. It had been a very long time since I was allowed to think of it that way. Not even a week after her last phone call to me, our leadership team contacted me to explain my own situation to me.

They said the terrible feelings were guilt, or distance from God. It was sinful to do gay things. Lying about it and the bad feelings that followed were a consequence of the distance that sin creates. The love I thought I felt was really 'codependence.' Women don't fall in love with each other, they only lust. Love would never lie for someone. Love only points others to God, toward holiness.

They called the sexual expression of that love deviant,

disordered coping. Isolated in a foreign country, I had perverted culture shock, codependence, bad coping, and deviant pleasures of the flesh into love and intimacy. The enemy had deceived me.

Those leaders were good people and they cared about me. They believed they were helping me recover. A part of me agreed with them. I did feel terribly confused. Tenderly brushing the hair from her face while she slept to kiss her forehead and whisper "I love you" could very well be sinful. Maybe sticky notes on the fridge affirming her beauty were sinister. Maybe stealing each other's journals to write paragraphs of mushy affection was from the Devil. Maybe those things were just wildly manipulative.

It's possible I could have misunderstood it all. I did lie. A lot. Sometimes I did distract her from doing devotions, afraid something she read would steal her from me. That is very selfish. It did feel selfish to get to be near her. I was spoiled with bliss after being tangled up in each other. They could have been right.

A strange peace filled my body as I accepted their message. I didn't love Laci. I wasn't a lesbian. I was just foolish and deceived. I welcomed their alterations, believing that it would restore me to the life I had before all of this nonsense. These memories with Laci truly didn't fit the rest of the album I had been creating. They were a different person, one that didn't align with the story being told. This had to be done. This would fix it. This would fix me.

The plan worked. It was just a matter of time before every sweet memory I had of us turned my stomach with regret. The pain I likely would have associated with simple heartbreak became the evidence that I had lived disobediently. If I had just done what God had asked, I wouldn't be sad, and I wouldn't be hurt. I was embarrassed that I had committed such a sad moral failing. Examination, confession and repentance were the only way to handle such atrocities. On the advice of the leadership team, I should tell my pastor what happened. He would be able to guide me back into good standing with the church, with myself, and with God.

Just the thought of this was mortifying. It was the same church that inspired me to burn my CDs. The same people still worked on staff. When I moved away, my parents started attending that church. They had developed a close friendship with the pastor, my pastor. The guy I was supposed to go to in penitent confession for my sexual sin.

His daughter Madelyn was a good friend, close to my age. He was a 55-year-old man. Was a 22-year-old woman really expected to share sexual content with a 55-year-old man? I tried rehearsing in my mind but couldn't construct any phrase that didn't send me into a full body blush of shame.

My parents joining an evangelical denomination with me was a bittersweet thing that grew less sweet over time. At first it was very exciting and I loved that they were a part of things. Dad was reading books about theology and would come to me with questions. In many ways I felt like I had some spiritual authority over him, a terribly uncomfortable seat to occupy. It was also a father and daughter enjoying a shared interest so it was fun and exciting. He came from a long line of ministers, men who had built churches, and I knew it made him proud to be turning out more like them. He was proud of me for turning out more like them.

The catch-22 was that they were also adopting the very tenets of faith that were coiling tighter around my neck. Up to this point, I had a unflinching confidence in the unconditional nature of my parents love for me. Could we be in a position where the church's authority could convince them otherwise? It was the first time I had wished they had just stayed Methodist. It felt too risky to just confess to them or to my pastor.

If I could practice with someone, that might help. Rosina, was the perfect choice. We moved in together as soon as I got home from Croatia and since my last call with Laci, she had developed a habit of asking me if I was okay. Not wanting to reveal too much, I brushed off her observed melancholy as the symptoms of a rough re-entry into my own culture.

One afternoon on the floor of our townhouse I gambled on her long track record of compassion and unleashed the truth.

"Ro, I need to tell you something but I don't want you to freak out."

"Um, okay, what's wrong? You're scaring me. Are you sick?"

"No no," I reassured her, "It's just, something happened and I feel like you should know about it." She did not look reassured. "So you know, my friend Laci that I told you about."

"Yeah, Croatia Bestie." She did *not* like Laci.

"Okay, well, some stuff happened between us. Some bad stuff."

"Did she hurt you?" She leaned closer, her eyes flashed a threatening rage.

"No no...umm...like dirty stuff...sexy stuff."

"Oh." Her back stiffened and she leaned back just enough for me to notice the growing distance between us.

"Listen, it was bad...like...I know it was bad. I feel terrible. That's why she called the other day. She told the team about us. They're kicking her out. She's going home next week."

Her eyebrows furrowed. She seemed confused, worried,

hurting.

"Umm... okay. So...are you telling me you're gay?"

"No! Absolutely not! We were just struggling. We were lonely in our living arrangements and it was just a terrible way to cope. It was like women in prison!" That wasn't in the script my leadership team had taught me. My eyes started filling with tears and I gnashed my teeth to try and hold them back.

She saw my fear and wanted to soothe it.

"You're like my sister, Jiggs. I love you. I mean, this is a big deal, and a lot to process, so I'm going to need some time. But I do love you and I'm so sorry you've been carrying this."

Tears streaked my face. Her comfort felt nice, but it also sounded like it wasn't the final word. She had to "process." That was another word that had grown more mysterious to me. Is it "process" the way we process bologna? Or process like a computer calculating what something means. Any way I could spin it, it meant people were going to be thinking about me when I wasn't there and drawing conclusions that could come back to bite me.

My revelation changed our friendship for a while. The changes were mostly my own paranoia. Her face wrinkled when she looked at me: it was either suspicion, judgment, or worry. She would walk lightly around the topic, asking if I had heard from Laci, unable to hide her relief when I told her I hadn't.

Telling Rosina had been hard, but it had been good practice for telling my parents. Dinner seemed as reasonable a place as any to air dirty laundry. Unable to get much of my meal past the lump in my throat, I pushed the food around on my plate to give the illusion that I was eating. I rehearsed the first line of my confession until the words no longer felt like words, then I opened my mouth to speak them. I told them the official story. Friend. Lonely. Scared. Blurred Lines. Big mistakes. Not gay.

They held open the room with a lot of kindness and compassion. They reassured me of their love and offered support, but were generally unsure of what they should do. I wasn't much help there. Telling them was as much of the plan as I had worked out. We agreed to just let it be. That had been our way historically and it worked for most situations.

My courage was still too insufficient to tell my pastor. I called a friend to schedule a lunch date. After driving an hour and a half I pulled into the parking lot of a fast food restaurant. Pam was already waiting for me. She was my older, wiser friend who had been my main source of encouragement toward missions. She hugged me warmly. We ordered some chicken and exchanged pleasantries. Then I dropped my bomb.

"I wanted to meet with you because some stuff happened when I was in the field." She sat calmly waiting out my confession.

"Living with a Croatian family was really hard and the stress was too much, I guess. I developed an inappropriate relationship with a teammate. It lasted for a while and then she," I let the pronoun do the heavy lifting, "told everyone about us and got sent home."

Tears showed themselves before I finished the last sentence. I was getting better at saying it, but still couldn't stop crying about it.

"I'm sorry this happened to you," she said flatly. "Can I ask why you felt the need to tell me?"

"I don't know. I guess I just felt like you should know. You were so proud of the fact that I went. I guess I feel like I let you down, not doing a better job." My mouth uttered that explanation but there was more that went unsaid.

Pam had a crooked smile, walked with a certain swagger, and played sports. You know what I mean? I think I was hoping I would hear something akin to, "Oh girl, me too, you'll get over this. I slept with three girls before I met my husband!" Pipe dreams. It was a brief fantasy that there was something normal about what had happened. That there were other people who struggled and found their way. It seemed pretty clear that I wasn't going to find it from her that day.

She, like everyone else, ended our talk with the same advice: I needed to talk to my pastor and get a good Christian counselor. They wanted me to figure this all out so it wouldn't happen again. That was, of course, a ridiculous idea because I knew I was never going to go overseas again, and I certainly wasn't going to live under that much stress with a beautiful and flirty Californian woman. How could it possibly happen again? This advice felt like hot judgment. They wanted me to go to counseling to figure out why my sexuality was so backward. There was nothing to figure out. I. Was. Not. Gay.

After about a month of knowing, Mom and Dad approached me admitting they were struggling. They really wanted to get some advice on how they were feeling and the best way to help me and asked my permission if they could talk to Madelyn's Dad. This felt like a sign to me. I was told I needed to tell him, but didn't want to tell him. Maybe they could tell him, and it would mean I didn't have to tell him. They had my blessing and could reach out for guidance and support.

When they told him, I guess he too needed guidance and support from his wife so he told her. Then his wife apparently needed guidance and support from Madelyn so she told her. It's unclear who Madelyn turned to for guidance and support as I took this horrifying chain of toppling dominoes as a sign to check the hell out.

As it would turn out, the pastor didn't know what to do with me. The advice he sent through my parents was that I go to the district superintendent of the church and tell him. He would definitely know what I needed to do to get back in good standing with God. Afraid of who that guy might turn to for guidance and support I decided my season of confession was done.

The truth of what happened was told to me and I accepted it. I accepted that I was dangerous and dirty and stepped out of the spotlight that had found me in college. I wasn't going to confess this to another person. Not the district superintendent, not a Christian counselor and not Jesus Christ himself. I stepped back into the darkness offstage, out of sight. I stepped away from the denomination that I had failed, preferring to accept separation as a just punishment for my crimes against them and God.

This was the end of this stupid story for me. I wasn't gay, I wasn't broken. I didn't need restoration, or fixing. I just needed the scrutiny to end and to start a new life. Give me the damn blank slate. I wanted to be left alone.

Brandi looked at me over her reading glasses. Her pen in her hand, a yellow notepad on her lap filled with black scribbles. Her eyes squinted in apology, mine darted to the floor.

"That's a painful story."

"Yeah."

"Thank you for sharing it with me."

My lips pulled tight against my teeth, a half-hearted smile.

"There's more though, it seems," she gambled, "Laci wasn't the only painful story."

I shook my head, eyes still fixed on the floor.
"Not even close."

# 10

# Adulteress

Five years had passed since Laci's great confession. Mary's husband was on the phone. He was crying.

"She's been in the hospital for a couple days. She's just not herself," he whispered.

"I'm so sorry, brother. I wish I could help," I said.

"I do need to ask you something. She...she's been saying a lot of things. Some of them are off the wall. But I need to ask you about one thing." He paused while he steadied himself.

*Fuck*, I thought. *Here it comes.*

"She says the two of you have been having an affair for a while now. I didn't know if that was true or not. I guess I just need to hear it from you."

I closed my eyes and felt giant tears splash on my knees. I could lie. She's in the hospital, he doesn't totally believe her. But when she gets better, she'll just tell him and then I'll look like an ass who lied right to his face. That's a worse predicament than the one I'm in right now, if that's possible. I have to just own this.

"Yeah man. It's true. I'm so sorry." I wept more obviously.

He was such a good guy. What possessed me?

"Um okay. Well," he said, "I really don't know what to say. So I'm just going to let you go. I'm a man of God so I forgive you as much as I can right now, and just ask that you don't contact my family again."

"Yeah. I promise…and thank you…and I'm sorry."

Silence bulged the walls of my apartment. My sexual brokenness had done it again. The burning humiliation was hotter this time, because what went on was much more obviously wrong. It wasn't young love. It wasn't innocent. It was horrible, adulterous, evil. The ripple effect of my relationship with Laci was tumultuous, but only rocked our boats. This was going to be more like a tsunami of destruction.

It all happened innocently enough, and genuinely I fought against it for a long time. I'd been living with Rosina, doing my best to put the story of Laci behind me. I was broke and facing adulthood for the first time on my own and I needed a job. My parents gave me a rapidly aging car and a predatory lender gave me a high interest credit card. The clock was ticking.

After a lot of failed efforts at entry level jobs, I sat despairingly at my dining room table looking at the stack of bills unsure of how to pay them as my available credit balance was being chipped away by things like rent and food. In a stroke of genius, I thought I would try and see if one of these places asking me for money might be interested in giving me some. That's how I landed a job at the cable company: the perfect gig to sustain me while I reinvented myself.

For a temporary job it was great. Days were spent keying in data and confirming work orders with customers. Most importantly, mistakes wouldn't ruin anyone's life. The work fulfilled me as long as no one in the cubicles next to mine exposed its futility.

Between actual work assignments, I would pull up blank fax machine templates on my computer so I could type out the accumulating pain swirling in my heart. Laci had once been my most intimate relationship but had become little more than a formally named black hole into which I sent endless correspondence. I deeply missed her.

Deep loneliness grew like vines up the stone walls I had built to protect the world from having to look at me. People were often kind to me, but no one could love me. I was at a new church; a different denomination. It was the same environment as before, except no one knew any of the horrible things I had done on the mission field.

My role as the sad quiet girl in the black leather jacket who occasionally played bass and sang backup vocals struck some people as cool. Cool and mysterious apparently vibrates at the same frequency as sad and distant. A few curious villagers lurked just outside of my vine-y walls, believing something wonderful existed inside. One such villager was Mary.

Mary was lovely. Older by a couple decades, she overflowed with casserole recipes and colorful anecdotes. She served me both warm food and loving-kindness with a large spoon. I met her one evening when I reluctantly attended a midweek Bible study.

The discussion was mediocre and a little boring. Try as I might, I couldn't resist the temptation to stroke my own ego by whipping out an intellectual piece of Biblical trivia. This did a number on Mary. She was immediately curious about me and chased me down with purpose. After a great deal of convincing I started having lunch with her regularly and before I could protest we were pretty close friends. With her help, I learned how to properly appreciate a sunset and find the best price on down comforters. For a grown up, she was pretty cool.

One evening, I was sitting in my car watching the sun dip into the lake and mulling over our budding friendship. My biggest fear was that her affection for me was the result of my manipulations. She thought I was a good person, but I had been fooling her. I knew what I was, and she should be allowed to know too. She wasn't a perfect Christian. She had secrets like the occasional cigarette and her love of the word shit. Maybe her affection for me wouldn't change. Evangelicals can be tricky. This sin is not like other sins. This could really push her away.

I waited until the sun had vanished below the horizon and made my decision. I'm going to tell her. Shifting my car into gear, I did something I never did, I paid her an unannounced visit.

My heart raced as walked down her long driveway and into the garage that was most always left open. I stood on red brick doorstep waiting to knock. It was only 8 at night, but I convinced myself that everyone was sleeping. They have dogs. If I knock, the whole house is going to erupt in chaos. This is dumb. I shouldn't do it. Crap, I couldn't just walk away. I was standing in their garage. If they notice me walking away, they would definitely think I was crazy.

My knuckle sheepishly rapped on the door. The dogs barked. "Ahh, crap," I whispered to myself. She opened the door and stood there in her pajamas backlit by the glow of the kitchen. Frozen in the doorway, I picked at my thumbs.

"I'm sorry it's so late and I should have called first, but I was wondering, if I'm not interrupting, can we talk?"

She looked genuinely worried and offered, "Of course, honey, come on in!" She offered a drink, or some cookies and I declined. I needed to do this before I changed my mind. There's no rest for the wicked.

She took me to the patio and sat me down. Then I began, "I want to tell you a story of something that happened overseas. I've never really told anyone except for the people involved at the time, but I feel like you should know. I want you to know."

"Okay, honey, let it out."

So I did. Like a broken levee I poured out everything that had happened to me, just as I had been taught to frame it. It came out naturally, well rehearsed, like it hadn't been two years since it had last been given breath. I apologized for not telling her sooner, for not being more honest about who I was and what I had done. What happened next to our friendship, I assured her, was hers to decide. We could remain friends, or she could kick me to the curb, I would understand.

All at once I fell silent. With tears in my eyes and shaky, sweaty hands, overcome by a tidal wave of shame I sat. My eyes focused down at the ground to give her privacy. When I couldn't wait any longer, I looked up to see she was crying. My eyes refocused on the lovely printed indoor/outdoor carpet, I was convinced her tears were bad news. My heart started racing as I waited for her first words.

"Wow," she said, "It's so crazy that you're telling me this."

"I know, it's probably very unexpected and way out of left field and you're probably shocked and disappointed and maybe I shouldn't have told you," I was blathering.

"No, it's crazy that you wanted to tell me this because the same thing happened to me and I've never told anyone. My own husband doesn't even know!"

Having played through the conversation in my mind several

dozen times before having it (as I usually do) I felt certain that I had prepared myself for every possible outcome. Sitting there across from her in her long flannel nightgown and slippers, this option had never occurred to me. She didn't have a crooked smile, or a swagger and she hadn't played any sports. I was dumbstruck, but elated. This was the kind of "me too" confession I had spent years longing to hear. All this time I felt like I was alone in my suffering, that I could never be normal. But here sat Mary, normal as can be. This was, like, some kinda miracle, right? Clearly, God had connected us on purpose. She could teach me how to be normal!

Stuttering between the elation of a common link and the somber condolences for her suffering, I asked if I could give her a hug. She obliged and we embraced in laughter and tears. We continued sharing stories until very early in the morning.

Everything I had wanted from the interaction had happened. She still loved me, she told me God loved me, she said she was glad we were friends. She also gave me the surprise bonus that my being open and honest had really healed a lot of very old shame in her.

She shared with me the next day that our talk encouraged her to tell her husband and they felt more connected than ever. It was the first sip of real purpose I had tasted in years. I couldn't have orchestrated a better outcome with a magic wand.

Our friendship grew. If I had a problem, she was the first one I would call. She sent me text messages and emails and cards. We had regular time together and were deeply invested in seeing each other happy. She was making me happy.

Rosina was not happy. She had watched the Laci shadow envelop me in depression. She made a safe place for my grief and stood in it with me even when she didn't understand it.

She had opened up her family to me to keep me from falling off the cliff of isolation and despair. When Mary showed up, I was magically "all better." Rosina didn't like it and she was not one to hold in an opinion.

"I think you're spending too much time with Mary," she said.

Still wildly conflict-avoidant I didn't voice my rage, but it was there. How dare she. I was offended.

"What do you mean?" I said with a casual lilt.

"You know what I mean, Jiggs. You're like, obsessed! You're over there all the time, you talk about her all the time. It's like you're in love with her!"

"What is that?! Is that a gay joke? Are you mocking me?" My skin felt hot and my finger tips throbbed. I wasn't sure if I wanted to cry, confess, or bite her head off, so I clenched my teeth to keep myself pacified.

"No," she sighed. "I'm sorry, I'm not saying that. I'm just saying it feels weird. It seems codependent."

Somehow that was worse. This was supposedly my best friend and she was attacking me with judgmentalism. Had she not understood the pain I described to her all those months ago? Had she not remembered the hurt people caused me by lecturing me about codependency and boundaries? Why would she take this approach?

I knew better than to be defensive.

"Rosina, I get it. You're probably right. We have been spending too much time together. We may have gone overboard out of excitement at everything we have in common."

"What could you possibly have in common with a 45 year old mom?"

She wrinkled her eyebrows and squinted at me as I talked. I told her about the shared history Mary had revealed to me.

She laughed in surprise at my story. She didn't see my new friendship as a divinely inspired appointment that could teach me about the path to being a normal wife and mom. She thought it was suspicious, and dangerous. She was incredulous that I didn't recognize red flags flapping all around me.

Deeply afraid Rosina was right, I couldn't let on. She knew me, and my stomach twisted to think I might be having another unhealthy relationship, but I didn't know how to override the drive to see Mary. It felt innocent enough to look forward to our next appointment. How happy should a friend make me? Should I fight against thoughts of her when I'm reminded of her by a song or joke? Should I turn her down when she extends invitations? I was excited to have a friend, and didn't want to lose her. I had to do this one right. I had to figure this out.

Why was it always me who was wrong? Maybe Rosina was harboring jealousy. She had been my uncontested best friend for almost ten years and now someone was out-pacing her. Clearly, that was the real problem. She didn't buy that theory when I said it out loud. We agreed to disagree.

On a weekend not long after, Mary invited me over to hang out. She was spending the weekend by herself and we could have a girl's night. Rich conversation kept us awake well past midnight, laughing and sharing. The later it got, the more horizontal we got, until we were sound asleep next to each other. In the growing light of the next morning, I woke to find my head resting on her. This had been the first time I shared a bed with another person since Laci, nearly three years.

It felt so comfortable there with her that I nestled in deeper. Her heartbeat sang to me, strong and steady, she slid her arms around me and my eyes grew warm with tears. Love sunk right into my spirit, straight from her chest.

We were both in twilight between sleeping and awake. Her arms were tight but her grip was relaxed. Safety and risk increased with synchronous intensity, matching our breath. I opened my eyes to search for hers. When I found them, she kissed me. As she did I could hear my hope shattering as all my fears were realized. It was the sound of my failure. Bad at friendship, clearly gay, I was bound for hell.

As I kissed back, I was faced with how frequently I had dreamt of doing so. Maybe this wasn't friendship. It was wrong. It wasn't what we should be doing. If I closed my eyes and forgot who we were, it was good. When reduced to lips and hands and heat connecting in a brief moment, it was right. How could I put a stop to it and get out of this situation? Did I want to get out of it? I lingered blissfully a few more moments and then broke the contact. Instead of making the same mistake as last time and blowing up and yelling, I chose to calm myself. I didn't want to hurt Mary by having her think I was offended or angry.

When I pulled away, she panicked, jumped out of bed and walked backward toward the wall clutching the collar of her shirt in fear and modesty.

"Ohmygod, Jiggs, I'm so sorry. I don't know what I was thinking. I should not have done that." She pressed a hand to her forehead searching for an explanation.

"Mary, it's okay. It was an accident, it doesn't have to mean anything." My words came out much cooler and smoother than last time I was in this situation. My ease pierced the noise of her fears. She looked at me. I watched the lust return to her eyes, possessed by the connection she had just uncovered, she wrapped her hand behind my neck to pull me back to her.

This was clearly her first dance with the push and pull that I had long ago grown to tolerate.

My conscious mind fought against the twitching in my muscles that wanted to press her harder into the wall. She broke away and continued unraveling. She presented her stats aloud to remind the room.

"I'm married. I have kids. I've not kissed another soul in 20 years. I'm almost that much older than you. You must think I'm a pedophile, or an abuser."

"Um, I'm 24. You're no pedo." Jokes sounded cool, breezy. That's what we needed to get through this.

"Really Mary, we're fine. It was a fleeting silly moment. We were confused in the twilight of the morning. This can be our little secret." How quickly a wretch returns to her shame.

She wouldn't forget. She meditated on it for a couple of days. She texted and called and met me in various places to tell me that she needed to tell her husband what happened. This was too bad. He deserved to know. I was completely opposed to the idea. Telling just gave it power. It forced us to consider what happened. This can't mean something. There weren't enough options to help define it. I wasn't under a lot of stress. I wasn't trapped in a bad life longing for a little bit of comfort. The only options required redefining myself, or admitting I was attracted to Mary. I already knew I was, but no one else did. Except for Rosina. She was going to be so smug if she learned what had happened. No way! I will not willingly crawl under society's microscope. Not again.

The tenacity of a devoted wife is unrelenting. This was her spouse. She had to tell him. My self-esteem spiraled. Who was I to stand between them and demand that she keeps this secret? We all know who I was: a nobody, a mistake. She never asked my opinion anyway. It wasn't my decision to make. It also wasn't my fault, she insisted. It was all hers.

She decided to tell him and sent a message to let me know moments before it happened. I was by myself and beside myself with worry that I was going to lose my friends again. My anxiety fueled visions of his future anger. He would blame me, of course. That made sense since it was entirely my fault for existing. He would rage at me. He might even hit me. At the very least he would banish me from their home and their family. As he should.

Several agonizing hours later, I heard from her. She was okay. He was okay. He wanted to sit with us and talk through everything. He wasn't mad, but he wanted to help us and protect us, so we definitely needed some rules. Rules would help. This didn't compute. I wondered if maybe she told the story wrong. Perhaps he didn't understand. At the end of such a revelation I should feel afraid, not protected.

Despite feeling protected, my fear was huge. There was an enormous burden to get this right and I didn't have the best track record. This relationship had to prove that I wasn't gay, and I was capable of platonic, boundaried, non-dependent friendships.

He dictated the terms. We couldn't spend the night together by ourselves. We couldn't be alone together for long periods of time, especially after dark. And her husband was allowed to read our messages on her phone whenever he asked to see them. I agreed, but his scrutiny was no match for my own.

I second guessed everything. Every touch, every text, every phone call was judged on its appropriateness, its relevance, its frequency. Every word with her needed to be necessary, holy, timely. Prayers filled my journals begging God for the wisdom to know when and where I should say or do anything. I prayed for protection, healing, clarity, wisdom, appropriate feelings, appropriate boundaries, appropriate emotional experiences. I prayed away thoughts of her. I prayed away missing her. I prayed away the sweet flowery smell of her.

The obsession to do the right thing was still an obsession with her. Every thought was still about her. All my effort was doing little more than painting her into a delicious, forbidden fruit. Occasionally, just before sleep, I would succumb to the temptation and be briefly beguiled by the fading memory of her touch. Just a little indulgence into what might have unfolded had we been otherwise inspired, otherwise obliged. And my conscious mind would dissolve into vivid, glorious dreams of her.

Nothing worked. God did not fix me. Our descent down the slippery slope had already begun. The rules became dragons we could fight to prove our love for each other. The presence of a dragon pulls the fight out of us long before we know if the princess in the tower is worth risking death. Watching someone slay dragons to climb the tower for a moment with us swells our hearts, before we know whether or not they are truly a noble knight.

Had her husband just recognized that I was the dragon he needed to slay, she would have felt the swell in her heart for him. Instead, I saw her multiple times a week, hugged her for too long and called her from my desk phone to avoid being caught. I felt every feeling I had felt in my relationship with Laci. I felt all of it right down to the aching in my fingertips. It was only a matter of weeks before we managed to leave town together for a beach weekend. By the close of the first night we had slept together.

It was the same dance as before, a constant two-step between wanting her and hating it. Holding her and hiding her. I want to tell you that I barely recognized myself, but it's not true, I knew this version of me. I knew her well. I hated her, but I kept becoming her. I was a liar.

Rosina persisted in confronting me with the unhealthy nature of my relationship to Mary, and every time she did, I doubled down in my defensiveness to protect myself from her truth. To try and appease her I told her about the rules we made with her husband. She asked what made us set up rules and I told her about the kiss. She froze in disbelief, barely able to tolerate the anger my disclosure generated in her. She was pissed at Mary for kissing me, Mary's husband for not protecting us better and me for not seeing how messed up it all was. Now she had evidence the whole thing was a cover-up and people were lying.

She was so mad, but it wasn't at me. She didn't see me as the same devil I saw in the mirror. She was mad for me. She talked about Mary like she was some kind of manipulative abuser. Her position sent me splitting into opposite corners of response. I wanted to defend Mary and protect her from being accused, but it was also the first time I considered that I might be a victim of some kind. How do adults victimize other adults? How would she have manipulated me into this position? Regardless of how we framed it, I knew it was bad. It was really bad in Rosina's eyes, and she couldn't even see the full picture. It devastated me when she stepped away from our friendship. But she was rightfully frustrated by my impenetrable denial.

She was more right than I could tolerate. She was wise enough to create a boundary to protect herself from a sketchy situation. It took an embarrassingly long amount of time to recognize that I was on the side of a boundary where the danger perpetuated.

# 11

# My Way

My eyes watered as they stared into the sun, watching it set over the sparkling waters of the lake. Mary and I were in the middle of another painful discussion. She had asked for some space to figure things out, but I had given too much.

"You don't have to cut me off completely. You can still text me and call me. You act like you're mad at me, or that you're relieved to not have to talk to me," Mary said with a tremble in her chin.

"I'm sorry, I don't know what I'm doing. I'm just trying to give you what you asked for. If I had my way I'd call you all the time. I'd never leave your side!"

That was true, sorta. If I had my way we would have been in constant dialogue and she would have a hard time getting me to leave her house. But my way would have also meant that she wasn't married and didn't have all the kids. My way would have been that we were the same age and looking forward to spending our entire lives together. It would have included not feeling like shit; like there was something wrong with me. She would have been a 24 year old man, for God's sake! The only times I even remotely enjoyed with her anymore were the times it was just the two of us –no one else around for miles. No one could find us, or out us, or judge us. Those moments were the only times I felt like things were going "my way."

Being around other people came with a tense twitching in my chest. I would constantly monitor my expression for any tells that I cared too much for her. Eye contact shouldn't last more than a couple seconds. Touches should only be brief and firm. Pats and thuds on the shoulders or kneecaps, pushes or pinches on the upper arms. Never soft, never gentle. Laughter should be loud and short. Never hushed, never giggled. Don't compliment her too much, especially about her body or clothes or hair. Stick to her character, or her cooking. Side with others when they complain to her, remind people that you don't care more about her than them.

When you go to her house, remember to act like a guest. Ask her husband for a glass, don't just pull them from the cupboard next to the fridge. Ask permission to have a cookie even though you know she bought them because they're your favorite. Forget that you know that the smoke detector battery needs changing and that they are out of creamer. You learned these things in secret meetings during the morning light, when no one else was there but the two of you.

No, If I had my way, we would live in an endless thread of solitude undisturbed by the observations of others. We would be suspended in the moments that we were forced to steal. Mornings when the sunlight shined bright and crisp through the curtains and cold air would dance over our bodies from the open window. Nights in my apartment lingering goodbyes, wishing you could rip the batteries from the back of time and space and stay there suspended forever. When it was just the safety of our own opinions and I couldn't be a deviant, or a disappointment. Those moments were so inviting that I did everything I could to make them happen, burning through paid time off as it accrued for just a brief taste of "my way."

One morning at work, my boss poked his head out of the office and called me to come sit with him. As I perched stiffly on the edge of a hard chair he shut the door behind him. He shifted some papers on his desk as he steeled himself to confront me.

"I wanted to talk to you about something I've noticed," he began. "It's kind of delicate and I just want you to know that I haven't talked to anyone else about this yet."

My eyebrows pinched above my glasses and my skin warmed on my neck. I held my breath as I waited for the hammer to drop. No telling where this was headed

"I've noticed a pattern in the days you call in sick and I'm wondering if there's not something more going on."

*No way is this how I get caught. How does he know? Why does he care?*

"I just want you to know that I recognized this because I've been there myself and there's no reason to feel ashamed."

Still stumped, I maintained my silence as I waited for the end.

"You've been taking off the Friday after payday every two weeks for several months. Do you have a gambling problem?'

The tension in my back released itself as I sighed a laugh of relief. "No boss, I don't," I chuckled, "I think that's just coincidence, but I'm touched that you worried about me. I'll try to be more mindful about when I take off days."

He leaned back in his chair, accepting my explanation and sent me back to my desk with a little business card that had the number for our company counseling line just in case I changed my mind or felt differently later. A smile hung on my face as I returned to my desk. It was funny that he thought I was a gambler. I didn't even know *how* to gamble.

Our conversation lingered with me for a while. I shirked off his worry so quickly because his conclusion was way off, but my behavior still resembled an addict: lying, hiding, obsessing, compulsing. Honestly, I was gambling. The stakes were high, and the house was going to win. The only way to survive was to stop playing the game.

Mary's anxiety in the car that day was spot on. When she asked us to back off, I was relieved. It wasn't the only feeling, sure, but I wanted this to end. As our relationship aged past months and years, the balance of pleasure shifted. The quiet moments were still good but lessening in frequency, diminishing under the weight of our effort to create them. Mountaintop experiences leveled by landslides. They were certainly no longer worth the prices we were paying. We were addicted and afraid. I didn't want to think someone could know me as well as she did and want to walk away from me. She was afraid that if I weren't attached to her I would expose her and she would lose everything that really mattered. Can you imagine accepting a reality where someone only clings to you as a kind of insurance against losing the ones they really love? That was not love. *That* was codependence. It was certainly not having it "my way."

Time moved on. Her house, that had changed from a light filled sanctuary of fellowship to a quiet little den of secret desire, was only filled with noxious vapors of disturbing memories. Moments once sweet and silly, spoiled by my own selfishness, soured and lingered in the air –the aroma of my brokenness.  Every piece of furniture, an unflinching monument to our indiscretions. Even her wall paper screamed of the sins it had witnessed. In my daily life, beautiful things would reach for me like they do for everyone. I would feel the warm light of spring or the refreshing chill of fall, but they were always punctuated with sinking in my stomach and a whispered thought in my unconscious mind, "this beautiful day isn't for you, it's for the good people."

With time, and maybe the final forming of my own prefrontal cortex, my guilt and pain thinned any pleasure in my relationship to Mary. Any love or tenderness had turned into an unquenchable yearning to be free.

# 12

# Queen City

In a merciful twist of good fortune, the cable company offered me a promotion that included a move and a relocation stipend. The distance would be good for me, and maybe good for Mary. I could still stay in touch and visit occasionally as it was necessary, and eventually we could fade from each other's lives. It was at least a different plan than the one we had tried and failed a hundred times.

At first, I felt alive with hope in the big city. New apartment, new job, fancy brand new car. Can we say *fresh start?* The pulse of the city invigorated my own. I joined an improv group and played guitar at open mic nights. The crowd's applause would wash over me, drenching me in approval. Their adoration was completely disconnected from my ability to be holy. Such a relief. That was also the year I met and fell in love with Taylor.

Taylor stood amongst a group of his brothers and sisters, the least enthusiastic of all of the basset hound puppies. Sitting perfectly content covered in a pile of the wriggling velvety soft droopy wrinkles of his siblings, he peered into my soul with his amber eyes and gave me a wink. A wink was all it took to know that sad ball of snuggle was my new best friend.

The first month of raising him was filled with joy and adventure. I don't think there is an animal on earth that can compete with the tender sweetness of a baby basset howling and tripping over his comically large ears. They are simply irresistible. He was so clumsy and charming. And he possessed an incredible power to make me laugh.

When we went for walks, people would be so visibly overcome with love for him they would cross ball fields and parking lots to squeeze him. It felt like positive attention for me to answer the questions of his fans, but I was clearly in his entourage and an ancillary character in his world, at best.

As he approached his first birthday, he traded his baby-face for a fat-boy saunter. He still drew a lot of oohs and ahhs from strangers but his projectile slobber and houndly stink shortened their visits and reduced the number of interesting questions. It wasn't long before we were the perfect pair and he was a great excuse to spend most of my time at home.

Along with caring for Taylor, I distracted myself from my past with music. I attempted to write new songs, but struggled. Everything I wrote sounded trite or untrue. It makes sense as I was lying my way through life. Lies don't sing. Church, on the other hand, was always a great creative outlet for making music. Mid-sized churches are almost always hurting for people with any small amount of skill and I loved seeing the relief I brought to worship leaders when I came to an audition as a new face.

Congregations enjoyed when I would sing. I still wasn't a soprano, so I could never be the lead female vocalist. That was okay. They were usually bubbly blonde women who wore the right clothes and could dance around the stage. That was not me. My voice and my style were much better suited for the "special" song that came right before the sermon. It was the pleading, groaning song of self deprecation and reaching to God for help. Heavy emotions were always trembling just below the surface for me. A little acoustic guitar in a minor key was just the elixir to bring them out for everyone to share in.

Playing in a church band also made it appear like you were in good standing with God because you were on stage, but you got to opt out of the sermons because you could say you were going to listen in at the 11am service, or pretend you had already listened during the 9am service.

Kindred spirits played there as well. The people talented enough to play at the level a church required tended to be former misfits from garage bands, or retired gig musicians. There would always be a story or two about someone's life before Jesus that involved drinking or drugs. Lots of these folks grew up in bars, playing for tips. There was sufficient gristle in my soul at that point that I could go toe to toe with their cynicism. We'd pass around stories to impress each other, but then furrow our brows in agreement that those were shameful behaviors of our youth.

In rehearsal one night, my church band leader struck up a conversation on 90s Christian music. Reminiscing alongside him, I mentioned how much I used to love Jennifer Knapp. He sighed and told me that he did too, but what happened to her was a shame. When I didn't follow, he enlightened me.

"My best friend is friends with Mac Powell, you know Mac Powell?" I nodded. Mac was the lead singer of Third Day, the originators of the first song I ever played live and the headliner for a tour that featured Jennifer Knapp. Mac was now apparently about to be the featured name-drop in a story that was definitely supposed to impress me. "Okay so my friend told me that Mac Powell told him that it was actually a scandal that made Jennifer leave music." He looked at me again, checking to see how ravenous I was for the dirt. I just waited and he continued. "She fell in love with her manager. Her *female* manager." He was unsatisfied with my level of shock. "She's a big ole'lesbian!"

My eyes rolled so far in my skull that I wondered if I would still need glasses. Maybe I rolled my eyes at him for the lame ass story. Maybe it was the blatant gossip. Gossip is bad. So what if she's gay? It sounds like she's happy. It has to be a pretty powerful love to leave behind millions of adoring fans and Grammy nominations. My hog-tied, duct-taped, inner lesbian was listening to the convo, absorbing his punches and raging to fight back. I was mad. Maybe I was mad at him for being homophobic. Maybe I was mad at Jennifer for possibly being gay. Or maybe I was mad that I stood there strapped into a guitar while listening to the tired old trope of female guitarists always popping up as gay. It's not gay to play guitar! Is it? Great. Now I feel gay for playing guitar.

When I got home that night, I did what I had done for years. I googled for the latest news on Jennifer Knapp. There was nothing. Not a sighting, or an open mic night. It had honestly never occurred to me that she might ever be gay, though it had occurred to me that she was hot. What if she were? It had obviously been made a black and white issue by the church. If she were gay she was gone, only the dust on a few albums to warn us that the same fate would befall anyone else coming out. What a waste; silencing such an enchanting voice.

Life was adequate in the queen city. A few creative outlets, a few new friends and my squishy little Taylor brought me hope that I could move forward. Mary was fading from my life as planned. She met and loved Taylor, but our relationship wouldn't last long enough for her to see him grow. Just when I started to believe that the worst might be over, her anxiety flared and soured inside of her until the fateful day that the truth of our whole torrid relationship gurgled from her throat and splattered all over both of our lives. Visions of the last time my secrets were broadcast on my behalf flashed before me, as I listened to her husband's heartbroken questions. As violating as it was to be exposed like that, I had no recourse, I had no right to be mad or hurt. I had done this to myself.

My heart teetered between moving on and digging myself into a pit. With deep relief washing over me that I didn't have to hide anything from anyone, I wanted to run around in freedom and finally feel happiness again. But I was still often weighed down by the shame of my own choices, laden with a fear that I was only capable of fucking everything up again. Though I was still in church, I was angry at God. Journals filled with fist shaking tirades at him for letting Mary into my life. It was his fault that I lost so much of my life in such a hole. He knew my heart, he knew what I could handle; how cornered I would feel and how I would cave to someone else's desires. What kind of monster would set up such a horrible test? I wasn't absolving myself for my choices, but I was pissed at the one who delivered such a slimy ultimatum.

At work I was doing my best to keep up with the pressures of a new role. My primary responsibility as a supervisor in the cable company was to be the main punching bag for irate customers. Most days I survived by staring at a model Volkswagon van I had on my desk, fantasizing about cussing out a customer, hanging up the phone, resigning and hitting the road as a traveling musician. I could write songs, play in bars and find temporary low-skilled jobs to earn enough money to get to the next city. These day dreams helped me get through the tough days at work, and provided an especially soothing release from the constant pounding of my own depression.

Eventually it occurred to me that the most important part of the fantasy was music. My depression was obviously a byproduct of miserable work, failed relationships and tragic mistakes. If I were doing something I really loved, or if I lived in a city that offered more opportunities to do the things I loved, surely I would be safe from making more horrible choices. This theory was so convincing that I opened up a special savings account and purchased a 1989 Ford Econoline van for $500 that I lined with purple carpet. My plan was to save enough to move to Nashville where I would constantly play music, build a community and either realize all of my wildest dreams of being a singer/ songwriter or find a confidence that I tried my best and those dreams were just not meant for me to realize.

My savings account got close enough to my goal amount that I started writing a resignation letter. It is my firmest belief that I would have submitted that letter and left for Nashville had Heather not come back into my life.

# 13

# Tempted

Heather was an enchantress. From the moment I met her on our first day at freshman orientation, I was captivated. She was an average girl in so many ways: average height, average build, average features. Unlikely to stand out in a picture full of other women for good or bad reasons, but her energy was infectious. Her aura radiated with so much vitality that she could make your skin tingle. Her sense of humor stole my breath and cramped my sides.

She met your eyes with confidence and curiosity. She regularly reinvented her style with the authority of a fashion designer. When her attention was on you, you felt like her best friend and the most interesting person in the world. When it ended, you wanted more. You can imagine my excitement when Rosina brought her back into my life nearly ten years after college had ended.

Rosina returned to our friendship after two years of formal distance. I was in the throes of a deep depression. It had been nearly a year since Mary confessed and her husband called to confirm. Basic isolation was my new coping mechanism.

It seemed safest to quarantine the mass population from my sinful diseases. I felt utterly poisonous, abandoned by God. My apartment was filled with cigarette butts, Diet Pepsi cans and the sound of Damien Rice's album "O" on loop. Thirty extra pounds of dense fat was padded to my face and torso, a repellant to anyone who might get too close. My relief came only from daydreaming about ending it all, either in death, or in running for the hills of Nashville.

Rosina had called to get relationship advice. Can you imagine? She was so anxious about her new boyfriend that she sought out the advice of a 30 year old virgin lesbian adulteress. Somebody get Alanis Morrisette on the phone, we found real irony. Dontcha think? No advice to Rosina actually passed my chapped and tar stained lips. Thankfully. I hadn't told her anything of my current state or the drama that had gotten me there, but she heard someone in that phone call she didn't recognize. She accessed her best friend-sixth sense and knew just what I needed. I needed a premier jewelry party.

She was inviting me to a multi-level marketing scheme she was going to host at her apartment. Christian women love multi-level marketing companies. They throw parties for handbags, hot scented wax, plastic storage containers, make-up, food processors, or nutritional supplements. This one was selling B grade costume jewelry and I was especially not interested.

"You need to get out," She persisted, "You don't have to come for the jewelry part, you can be fashionably late. There will be food and drinks and some of my favorite people. Then when they leave we can get all the gossip from Heather. She's coming! You love her!"

Yes. I definitely loved her. It would feel so nice to be in her aura. I had been so lonely and depressed. Maybe costume jewelry and a reunion were necessary. I was scared Heather had heard gossip about me. She was popular and connected. What if I wanted to see her and she wanted nothing to do with me. I couldn't predict the outcome, so I just went for it.

There she sat, cross legged on Rosina's couch, like no time had passed. Her back straightened and her mouth fell open with a gasp when she saw me. She patted the space next to her demanding that I sit and I fell into her waiting hug. Her warm greeting gave me such relief, I buried my tears in her shoulder to hide them. With so many other listening ears we padded the conversation with small talk. Since college she had gotten married, worked for a bit, and was now staying at home with young kids. That much ordinary was never something I would have predicted for her. She asked about my work, and swooned over pictures of Taylor. As the other ladies sauntered out, we met in the corner to take the conversation deeper.

"I was trying to think of the last time I saw you and I think it was at your going away party right before you left for Croatia."

"Oh, yeah, Croatia, yeah," I was not thrilled to hear the word.

"Yeah, tell me about it! Was it so great?!" She asked like she didn't already know.

"I will say," I replied, "It was the best time and the absolute worst time of my life."

"Oh really? What do you mean?"

"I mean, I loved being in a foreign country and playing music, and everything felt new and alive. But I made a lot of bad choices and got in some trouble." I had been assuming she knew as I really believed that the whole world was talking about me when I came home, but she kept looking at me with a furrowed brow like she was terribly confused.

Genuinely curious, she asked, "You made bad choices? That sounds interesting."

I still didn't buy her ignorance of the whole thing, so I was direct. "Do you really not know?"

"Nope," she said, shaking her head. "I have no idea what you're talking about, Jiggs."

"Well..." my hot shame cooled, but was immediately replaced with anxious nausea. Am I about to say this outloud? It seemed like a risk. Heather could reject me. She was a good friend, maybe she wouldn't. Really though, after Mary, the Laci story didn't even make me flinch.

"I slept with a teammate ... a girl ... uh... yeah. It was a bad idea. I finished my term, but she got kicked out."

She smirked as she narrowed her eyes at me. "Did you really." It wasn't a question. Her smile seemed to flirt with me, but that didn't make sense. I shook it off. We danced together around the subject, a few questions from her, vague answers from me. Her eyes never let go of mine. Her gaze told me she could see me, and still cared about me. Eventually, we changed the subject, but she continued to occasionally squeeze my forearm with her cool hand. Undoubtedly, a reassurance that I am not disgusting.

At the end of the night, she placed her phone in my hand and ordered me to put my number in. My skin grew hot. My thumbs trembled as they searched out the numbers. I was being weird. Cleansing breath. Flashing a casual smile, I placed her phone back in her hand and felt her fingers brush against mine. I shouldn't notice this. Her arms reached upward and around my neck pulling me toward her. My hands knew to pat her back with a platonic pulse. My stomach kissed against hers and sensed a familiar hunger. My anger with myself grew and dismissed the chemistry as my own dysfunction. Cut it out, Jiggs. Perv.

Mid morning the next day, the screen on my phone lit up. My heart pounded. A text from her. Just small talk, though, she wasn't flirting. That idea was made up and ridiculous. I'm totally over it. After texting back, I pushed my phone away and punished the gum in my mouth while attempting to refocus. Between keystrokes I would glance at the notification light. Nothing. I was distracted. I needed some movement.

My fingers pushed around the change in my desk drawer counting out enough for a drink. I abandoned my phone to walk to the soda machine. The bubbles burned my throat as I stayed in the breakroom to take my first sip. A brief chat with the receptionist about her dog was a refreshing dose of reality. I'm not obsessed. Self discipline inspired me to take the long way back, checking on my employees, looking out the window. Was that a new statue in the courtyard? My drink came to rest on my desk with a thud. The message light blinked. Delight filled me. The conversation had begun.

We slid downhill together effortlessly, first through pre-pubescent boy humor, then into double entendres. By the time we reached secret confessions I knew the signals I was picking up on yesterday weren't just the fault of my broken radar. She was increasing the temperature to a sultry heat.

When she demanded the full details of my stories, my thumbs feverishly clicked the tiny letters on my blackberry obediently delivering. Questions would interrupt my narrative begging for more detail. Inspired by her longing, I drew her more intimately into my stories with compelling imagery. Masterfully, I articulated all of the saucy, scandalous intricacies of not one but two star-crossed love affairs. Each phrase was carefully crafted to tilt her hips forward in her chair and send a blush up the back of her neck. We rode the full length of the slippery slope and I made sure it was extra slick.

When I reached the last page in my catalog of erotic tales, I called her and demanded reciprocity. She deflected, insisting the stories she could tell were boring married people stories. The better ones she wasn't at liberty to share with just anyone.

Well, well, well … what a sexy little breadcrumb you've left for me here.

"What do you mean better stories? Do you know good stories about other people?" bait taken.

"No, I mean, I don't know if I can trust you enough to tell you some of my stories because they involve other people's *secrets*," she cranked the reel.

"I see, I see, I pour out my heart and give you all my best stuff, other people's secrets included, and you're denying me on a technicality," I'm totally hooked.

She hesitated, then proceeded to tell me that she had been cheating on her husband for a couple of years with her best friend, her best girlfriend.

Jackpot.

Not surprisingly, our conversation devolved even further until we were painting vivid fantasies of one another. Each of us upping the ante to scare or intimidate the other into our separate "good girl" corners. She slid all her chips into the pot by inviting me to meet for dinner at a restaurant between us. It was my first real date with a woman. I mean, she was flirting with me, and she asked me to dinner. That's a date. I stressed over what to wear and chose something specifically to accentuate my cleavage. That's a date. I put on eyeliner, for God's sake. That's a date.

We stared at each other with a sexy laughter in our eyes, seeing each other for the first time in a new light. Every joke was a tease and every eye contact lingered. We were both day dreaming of bad decisions, but adamant we would only enjoy the fantasy. Wherever she moved, I stood too close. A graze of her arm with my hand brought out fire in her skin. Holy shit, was I flirting? I didn't even know I could do that! Our hug goodbye was electric and lingered, but it was only a hug. Before either of us could get settled back in our houses we were texting again, sharing all of the things we were thinking and feeling in the hours prior. All of my flirting actually worked; she had received every message loud and clear. It was exhilarating to combine the tension of a date with the inside scoop of a friend. This could spell trouble.

Perhaps some of you are wondering if I am really going to be this easy, this thick-headed. It had been two years since the world fell apart after Mary. It had been nearly ten years since it had fallen apart after Laci. Am I incapable of learning a lesson? Maybe I'm just comfortable with destruction. It could be that I just hadn't built anything worth protecting since the last rupture. I knew I was about to do something stupid. Nearby seismometers could pick up on the approaching earthquake. But all the warning bells in the world were no match for the insatiable force within me. I wanted that girl.

No time had passed before we found ourselves meeting again. Sitting in my car in a shopping mall parking lot, both confessing that we were tempted by each other and disclosing all our thoughts, we casually sat on the brink of a highly consensual relationship. She sat across from me with all the confidence of someone who had pushed all her chips into the center before, but never lost the hand. She didn't know what it felt like to watch the dealer callously rake in your life savings. The irony of the moment is that I did know, and still sat there ready to play another hand.

After a cleansing breath I connected to her gaze and, without looking away, reached for the button to release my seatbelt. The strapping slid through my fingers as I leaned toward her, my eyes fluttering in a dance between her eyes and her mouth. I had dreamt of this for years. My hand reached to cradle her cheek. I drew her face close to mine slowly as the potential of our first kiss lingered somewhere in the heat of our mingled breath. We paused there to steel our intention and to allow the growing electricity between us to reach its peak. Spanning the distance between us felt like a climb, but once our lips touched, everything that came next was as easy as falling off a cliff.

# 14

# Endings

My toes dug into the surface of the rock. My eyes darted from the water to my feet in an effort to calculate how far away it was and thus how long I would be free falling before I reached it. My life-jacket squeezed my torso causing my arms to lift from my sides. A bead of sweat ran down the back of my neck. Life was hot up on the rock.

"Are you sure about this?" I cried out.

"Yeah dude, haha, it's like eight feet, ten max. It's nothin. You got this." shouted Kristen as she bobbed in the murky water below. She had just completed her third jump to demonstrate the safety of the task before me.

"What if there's a giant rock below the surface that you didn't hit because you're little but I will hit it and fracture my spine in three places rendering me a quadriplegic and I'm forced to give motivational speeches for the rest of my life?"

"The odds are low, but never zero. But my friend Ricky jumped from there last summer and he's bigger'n you. He was fine. C'mon! Do it!"

Kristen was an expert on badass behavior. I had met her

several years earlier at Heather's house. She was playful and brassy. Her face was dotted with freckles and her hair usually pulled into a high pony ready for adventure. Her eyes sparkled delightfully and an inner daredevil often tugged at her smile. She was considerably younger than me, a fact which would blush her freckled cheeks with defiance if I brought it up too often. She was an old soul, she insisted. She demanded respect. She could smoke a cigarette like a 45 year old woman. Our friendship was built around our shared interests of hiking, camping and kayaking and was now convincing me to jump off of this cliff.

I had made the foolish mistake of complimenting her courage and requesting that she design a curriculum to help me become a badass just like her. She not only obliged, but created a really specific check list of obstacles to put me through that upon completion would absolutely certify that I too was a badass. This jump was on that list. Staring down at the sparkling water below it occurred to me that perhaps it wasn't Kristen's courage that made her a free spirit but rather her age that left her lacking important parts of her brain that made her seem free, but really she was just reckless.

With clenched fists I curled my arms like a runner in mid stride, took one step backward and shifted my weight forward stepping off the cliff and into thin air. It had been my plan to scream a "Waa hoo hoo hoo" like an old Goofy cartoon as I flew through the air, but the fall was so short I just got a "Waa" before the water rushed around my body. When I surfaced, Kristen was cheering and excited that she got it on camera.

"Oh my god, you finally did it! I thought you were gonna pitch a tent up there! Good job dude, that was real badass!"

By the time we reached the cliff diving phase of our friendship, we had already spent what amounted to months together camping and hiking. Dangling in hammocks in the dark woods leaves a lot of room for conversation, and she and I had long since confessed every secret we had. She even knew about Mary. I remember feeling apprehensive about sharing that story in particular. Kristen was a lot younger and I toyed with the notion that it might not be good for her to know. It was that level of protectiveness over Kristen that revealed to me the darker sides of my relationship with Mary. I was afraid of corrupting Kristen's young life with a story, what force would have been capable of motivating me to touch her? Never being able to imagine doing such a thing to Kristen made me wonder what possessed Mary to reach for me the way she had. That affair made me wonder if I was capable of having boundaries at all. But my friendship with Kristen proved that I not only could, but really enjoyed it. Kristen was also a great friend in helping get over Heather.

For nine solid months Heather and I had poured all of our energy into materializing every fantasy we could conceive. They were good. I mean, you know, they were bad. They were illegal in some states. I had activated a side of me that I didn't even know existed and I was kind of impressed. In that relationship, I was a badass. Every time we met it was something new. It was fun and dangerous and dirty, and, for a few months, I loved it. Months of steamy clandestine rendezvous and salacious weekends spent together definitely feed the ego. But I had a problem. I wasn't just brazenly objectifying her and casting her aside. I was falling in love with her. I missed her. I thought about her constantly. I longed for a text or a call. I watched her sleep and brushed her hair away from her face. Our fast and sexy relationship normalized into a calmer, more complex intimacy. I loved Heather in the way that I would do anything for her, and if she left her husband, I would gladly spend forever with her. I wondered about the love she felt for me. It seemed more like buddy love that wants the best for you, and wants to help you find what you long for, but doesn't want to BE what you long for.

My love for her seemed like a bad side effect, the blister you get from your favorite pair of shoes. You love the shoes, you look adorable in them, but wearing them always hurts a little. She cared about me, and I believe it hurt her to think our relationship was hurting me. But, like any good pair of shoes, I tried to conform, afraid she'd just stop choosing me if I made things uncomfortable.

Decentering her from my universe worked. I persisted in convincing both of us that my only actual desire was to fall in love with a man and build a family and live happily ever after. This strategy gave her relief that I wasn't getting too attached and helped me believe that the pain I was experiencing was temporary. Heather often fielded my questions about what men were like, if they compared at all to women. When my face looked concerned enough, she would comfort me with reassurances that men were just like women. They could be soft and sweet. They could smell good and be compassionate. She regularly slept with both and found both experiences enjoyable for many of the same reasons.

Once, in her pantry looking for a missing ingredient, she met me and pulled the door behind her to keep her kids from spying. My pulse quickened believing she was about to pounce on me. Her eyes were more calculating than lusty. The way she was clutching my arm signaled that she had something important she wanted me to know. With unwavering eye contact and stern gravity she said in a low voice, "If you decide you're gay, that'll be okay." Embarrassed by how soothing it was to think that might be possible, I felt my eyes burning with tears and could hear an echo of a voice deep in my mind whispering, "for you I would be." But I didn't say that; I couldn't. It was fruitless to long to have her to myself. She was as devoted to what she had created as I was to finding the same for myself. She enthusiastically accepted my request to help me set up my online dating profile.

She sat close to me at her computer as I made my way through the prompts of the dating site. She would nod to affirm each click along the way. Eyes: Blue. Build: curvy. Height: tall. Seeking: men. She elbowed me out of her way and slid the computer in front of herself to select my pictures. I didn't know my best features nearly as well as she did, so her opinion was most important. After uploading pictures she started asking the open-ended questions.

"What's your idea of a perfect first date?"

"Umm, I dunno, dinner?"

"Noooo, c'mon, that's boring, you gotta be a little spicier!" she insisted. She typed as she spoke.

"Nothing too formal. Drinks and conversation. Dinner if we click. If we're lucky...dessert."

"Ohmygod, you're insane." My skin crawled thinking about some strange man reading that and thinking I said it.

"What? That's flirty! Guys love that stuff!" She rubbed her hands together, "on to the next one!"

We sat there together question by question, constructing the perfect dating profile. We used me only as an inspirational starting point, the bulk of the content was just clickbait wrapped in sexual innuendo. By the time we got to the part where you could actually shop for men, she was ravenously pouring over their pictures, liking and rejecting them at will. To her credit, she tried asking me if I liked them, but the thought of clicking that button made me feel ill. What if they talked to me? What if they asked me out?

A part of me genuinely wanted my prince charming to be among their faces. It would be nice if I could get through this crazy chapter of relationships with women and start building a real life. But I could have carried on forever just watching her have fun helping. She was handing me boys like garments over a changing room wall and having such a good time. I loved it when she had a good time.

The profile she helped me construct was so forward and flirty that I ended up not getting many dates from it. The fear of having to deliver on such teases made me too queasy to interact with anyone it baited. I privately built other profiles on Christian dating sites, preferring to interact with men in good Christian ways. Things didn't go well there either, though and that made me suspicious.

I would never have called myself superstitious, but there were elements of my faith that lent themselves to superstitious thoughts. One Sunday while sitting in the greenroom of my church passively listening to the sermon on a small tv alongside the other members of my church band, the pastor started talking about reasons we might find ourselves stuck in our lives. He poured over stories of the Israelites in the wilderness and how they basically journeyed in circles for years. It was not because the destination was far away or hard to reach. It was more because God didn't find them fit to enter the promised land they sought. God kept them away because of their disobedience. He held them back because their hearts weren't pure. They weren't ready. I sat there on that dirty little thrifted couch feeling embarrassed and ashamed. I hadn't found who God wanted for me because I was wildly disobedient. That wasn't superstition, that was just the daggum truth. I was out here playing the dating game with nice church boys who were in the market for a good wife. Even a bad Christian knows the attributes of a good wife.

According to the last chapter of Proverbs, a good wife is many things. She is industrious and thrifty. She is good at asset management and efficient with the running of a home. She is trustworthy with even the smallest things and everything she does brings about good for her husband and family. According to the book of Timothy, a good wife is submissive and quiet. She loves her husband and honors his leading of the family. She embodies prudence, temperance and beauty. According to obnoxious youth pastors she is also smoking hot and loves to have sex, but not until she is married.

Proverbs is also clear on the opposite of the virtuous woman. That woman is affectionately called the adulterous woman. She is a temptress whose way leads to treachery and death. Never get mixed up with the likes of her, God clearly warns. She's bad news. She's at worst a venomous spider, at best a chewed piece of gum.

If I ever wanted to have any hope of being a good man's wife, I had to put an end to the secret parts of my relationship with Heather. I wasn't winning with guys because I was a bad person. As soon as I fixed my character flaws, I would be good to go.

For a while, I could only fantasize about ending things. We could let go of each other. We could both choose the right path and denounce what had been going on. We both believed in

God, and we talked about faith regularly. We had been able to agree that this was wrong. We both wanted to be good people. I wanted her company on the highway out of Hell. We could stay friends, we could still hang out, we could still make memories, we simply couldn't stay in a sexual relationship. I thought it was a brilliant plan.

"Are you okay? Something's off."

We were sitting in her kitchen. The dishwasher was open and water was running in the sink. She had just wrestled a big casserole dish into the bottom rack and was drying her hands.

"Yeah, I'm okay, I dunno…" my chin wrinkled fighting back tears.

"Hey, what's going on?" she moved in close, the smell of dish soap lingering on her hand as she touched my face.

"I think I have to be done with us," I said, tears now tumbling from my lower lashes.

"Done with us? Done with me?"

"No, no. I mean, I'll never be done with you, we're forever. You're one of my favorite people. I think…just done with the bad parts of us. The dirty parts of us. I just want to be your best friend, you know? I want us to be sources of light in each other's lives. You know? I want to lift you up and I feel like I'm tearing you down."

She was sitting beside me now, fingers now toying with the dish towel. Her brow furrowed and she pursed her lips in an exaggerated frown.

"You don't bring me down, Jiggs. You're my favorite part of the day! If I'm down it's because I choose to be down. I bring myself down. You have never done that."

"I just don't think I can keep going. I feel like it's keeping me from finding what I long for. I feel like God is mad at me about us and is preventing my future from starting until I let you go."

"Well," she said, "You gotta do what you think is right. I would never want to force you. If you need to stop, that's okay. We can stop."

As soothing as the discussion was to the guilt ridden part of me, it devastated me that she could just let go so effortlessly. She was also good at not sharing how hard things were on her. For all I knew it was catastrophic. My heart tossed around feelings like salad in a bowl. I was relieved that it was drawing to an end, already grieving our intimate connection, sad that she would let me go, mad that it had to be done.

It took some time. My convictions weren't strong enough to cut her off cold-turkey. But guilt flowed more consistently than it ebbed and eventually we stopped. Well...I stopped. She didn't stop. She needed the bad side too. There were parts of her that she wanted to let loose, and having a girlfriend did that for her. Yeah, it was bad. But, she reasoned, she would likely do something much worse without it. So, in the midst of me stepping away (which she honored and accepted), she replaced me with someone else.

She didn't call me one day and announce that she had moved on and met someone else. It's not like I went to her house, and she introduced me to someone and said, "This is my new secret girlfriend." This is, of course, not how secret girlfriends work. A careful observer would notice the same name frequently popping up in Heather's stories. At first it was grouped on guest lists for cookouts and parties. Then it was added to more intimate dinner parties and trips with the ladies' Sunday School class. Then she started inviting the woman to things that were supposed to be just the two of us.

After driving all the way from out of town for an afternoon with her, there sat Miss New Bitch, at the dining room table with all the children. When I would call to chat, I would hear New Bitch in the background. Her plans for the day included New Bitch and her little bitchlette children. I'd ask about a weekend to go hiking or camping: nope, sorry, I'm going to get tattoos that weekend with New Bitch. How about the next? No. Me and New Bitch have concert tickets.

"Oh, sure, cool," I murmured into the phone, "sounds great, hope y'all have fun."

"What." she inquired, "What's wrong with you?"

"Are you and whatserface fuckin or what?" I snapped.

"What are you talking about? Who?"

Hmph. Like she doesn't know what I'm talking about.

"Way to dodge the question, I know you guys are fucking. Just tell me! Why you gotta lie?"

"Umm, first of all, no. Second of all, why do you care? Would you really want to know if we were?"

Oh they were. I knew they were. Heather couldn't share a hotel room with someone and *not* sleep with them. I knew her, I knew how she played people. I knew how she caught people. And now she was fucking lying right to my face.

"I know you, Heather. I know what you do. Don't you even care about who you might hurt? Isn't this girl married too? Man, what kind of people are you?"

"Wow. Okay. You know, you and I were fucking two weeks ago...so...whatever kind of person I am, you are too. And you know what? I gotta go...I can't with this."

She hung up the phone without saying goodbye. There was definitely no "love you" at the end either. I knew I was being a dick. Seeing your behaviors from outside of the thrill was really illuminating. I was attacking her, but sick with myself.

Sleeping with someone else hurt my heart, but it wasn't the worst pain I was experiencing. She had once treated me as her highest-ranking secret keeper. I knew her better than anyone. Mine was the one and only VIP pass to her inner world. Just weeks ago, she was sharing every thought and activity no matter how mundane or naughty. From her plans for the afternoon, to the deep fear and guilt she felt about who she was becoming, I knew it all. But now, suddenly, I felt like a prince banished from the kingdom standing alone across an alligator infested moat, the drawbridge locked and secured. My access to her was relegated to glimpses of her silhouette in the tallest tower, backlit by candles, moving on in her life without me.

Having loved and lost only one other person by that time in my life, I was devastated. Laci had left me for God and holy living. That was painful, but at least I respected it. Heather left me because the shoes didn't fit; someone else better suited her life, so I was out. Everything had changed when I only wanted to stop cheating. The thought of someone else getting everything drove me mad.

All the guilt and all the shame I was carrying rotted in my stomach like spoiled cabbage. The only thing that tempered my pain was my righteous indignation toward Heather. No matter how bad and disgusting I was, she was more so, because she was still there. I could heave some of the fiery coals resting on my back right over the fence at her. She deserved them much more than I did.

I would twirl the thought of telling on them between my fingers like a poker chip. It would have to include a confession and that would be a gamble, sure. If I won the bet, people would see my confession as noble, restore me, love me, and help me. Then our collective judgment could rest where it belonged, on the backs of the women still cheating and we could all shame them together. If I lost the bet though, people would hear my confession and see me as diseased, disgusting. Why would I allow my perversion to break up two people in a sacred, committed relationship?

Years I spent torturing myself by staying in her life hoping I could change her. Maybe I was staying close so that I could be around when they fucked up and got caught. I wanted the fire of God's justice to rain down from heaven right in their laps. God's judgment had scared me away from that life, and I never saw it come for them.

There is a chance that this is not actually how God works. God doesn't out everyone. God doesn't humiliate the wicked. God probably loved them even though they didn't seem to give two shits about him. It wasn't fair. Eventually, I scraped up enough self-respect to call it a spade and walk away.

Initially, I left that relationship for what felt like noble reasons: honesty, integrity, justice, and inner peace. When she didn't follow me out, I was crushed. I found myself racing even faster back toward the faith I had all but abandoned for the encouragement to keep walking away. From the outside, I could pretend that too was noble. I was repenting and returning to God –a long-lost prodigal daughter. Wasn't I so brave? Wasn't I so righteous? No, I was smug and mean and wildly judgmental. I was self-righteous and petty. But the path was clear.

# 15

# Chicago

"You're not ashamed of your sexual identity, are you?" asked Brandi.

We had processed my three relationships with women and my sparsely populated experiences with men. She knew how much I loved the women I had discussed and how deeply my church guilt had camped out in my chest. Two years of therapy school also informed my incredulity for the question. She had asked it all wrong. She was leading me to the answer she wanted. Of course I responded correctly.

"No, of course not. I've worked through all of that," a partial truth.

"Tell me how."

"Well, I had a lot of time to think about things when I lived in Chicago." I began.

The numbers were accumulating in my 401k. Nine months remained before the cable company would start matching my investments, and I would qualify for a pension. Where I come from, it's an impressive thing to have retirement planned out in your 30s. The nine years I had spent there had been a tumultuous cycle of highs and lows. I was given raises and promotions, some better than others. They relocated me to a bigger, better city. I had moved from the front lines of the company, staffing calls from irate customers, to a softer position in the learning and development department. I taught a fresh class of new hires every few months. These people were excited to have a new job and not yet beaten down by the flurry of punches customer service could throw. I had so much going for me. I should have been proud. I wasn't. A stable job, savings and a nice car are nothing without purpose. My friendship with Heather was as withered as a flower in the fall. I was longing for a big change that would spur me toward purpose and meaning.

Madelyn had meaning to spare from the life she had forged in Chicago. Madelyn was my pastor's daughter at the church I attended in high school. She was four years younger than me and had an older brother just a year younger. In the 11th grade I feigned a crush on him because he was slightly taller than me, and a good christian kid. To improve my odds with him, I spent more time around church and his family. A credit to his intuition, my "crush" never went anywhere, but my friendship with Madelyn was born. She had always said I felt like a kind of big sister to her, something she was in deep need of after having lost her own at an early age. I felt protective of her and since I was the youngest in my family it felt good to have someone to watch over and give advice. We often laughed at how frequently she seemed to follow in my footsteps. She played basketball in my old number, attended the same university and even spent time in the Balkans doing missions shortly after I left. We lost touch while she was there and I had always told myself that it was because of what I did while

I was in Croatia. It was more likely that we were just grown ups living our grown up lives.

After she returned home from the mission field, she moved to Chicago. She had been there for almost a decade and had started a ministry with the unhoused population. I wasn't sure there was much friendship remaining between us, but something in my heart inspired me to check in and see how she was doing. Unexpectedly, she invited me to visit and experience her ministry while we spent time catching up.

In the wake of my relationship with Heather, I started reading a lot of spiritual books again. While I had been away being self-indulgent, a new kind of Christian was emerging: The Radical. These cats were cool, the hipsters of Christianity. They took Jesus seriously and sold everything they had to live in poverty and reach people for the gospel. They lived in communes and studied Scripture and the words of our forefathers voraciously. They had dreads and wore homemade clothes. They bought one pair of shoes and kept them until they fell off. They loved the planet and wanted to be good stewards of it and protect it. They were real and honest.

They brought back the memory of who I'd wanted to be when I left America the first time: all in and wildly committed. They even resurrected parts of me that existed before the small-town church shook all that beautiful dirt off of me. They didn't try to be like everyone else. They allowed Jesus to make them different. In fact, the status quo was probably sinful. They were hippy, progressive, liberal, social justice warrior Christians. Maddie was my passport to that life.

Before the weekend was up, I was submitting a resignation to the cable company and advertising a massive yard sale. Her life there had inspired me so much that I was ready to give up everything for a chance to join her.

"I'm not easy to live with," she warned, "I'm difficult and particular and it probably won't be as awesome as you're imagining." She stood in front of me, one of the few women I knew tall enough to meet my eyes squarely, offering me a blunt and bold way out. But I didn't bite. I knew this girl, I had known her since she was 10. You couldn't convince me that I would discover anything that I couldn't handle.

"That's okay Maddie, I'm easy going to a fault, so it's cool." I thought I was reassuring an insecurity, but was really ignoring a stern warning.

Summer heat was still warming the pavement when I got there in early autumn. Chicago was big and intimidating, but happy to see me. Regardless of my wealth of experience at relocating, a new city is always daunting. I arrived with a desperate pressure to learn my way around and mitigate my anxious vulnerability. My family had brought me, so we hit the highlights: Wrigley, the Bean, architectural boat tour, Second City, hot dogs and deep dish. The novelty was giving me life. By week's end, one couldn't distinguish me from a life-long Chicagoan headed to work on the L. My affection for that city grew deeper and more quickly than I imagined it could.

Madelyn was right. She was tough to live with. I had Taylor, who never made things easy. He was not her favorite addition. I'll give her credit that she tried to see his intrinsic value: he was very charming and disarming. There are few people that can resist the droopy pitiful jowls of a handsome basset. He sure was gross though. Bless his heart. I knew that. Bathing him regularly only animated his fragrance and the house smelled like we collected dead squirrels we pulled from car washes. The less money I had, the less often I could buy treatments for ear infections. So on top of houndly cornchip musk was a fungal yeasty cheddar. Oh, he was gross. With each of her complaints, I was filled with deeper shame and my heart broke for him.

Not only was Taylor a pain in Madelyn's ass, I too gave her plenty of suffering. I didn't wash my share of the dishes. When I vacuumed, I was supposed to take the throw rugs out and shake them. She didn't believe anyone had actually taught me how to scrub a toilet when I did such a terrible job at it. And she shuddered at the presence of my hair in the tub. With every passing day I collapsed on myself like a wadded up ball of paper. Just like I had done years before in the Croatian lady's apartment, I spent more and more time in my room, or out in the streets riding my bike or the train. In Croatia I grew more and more embarrassed with each word I didn't understand. In Chicago, my humiliation was compounded by every word I did.

It was a disaster, but I would persevere. This was, afterall, supposed to be a radical experience. Sometimes those can be painful and I shouldn't be such a self-involved capitalist about everything. So I'm uncomfortable. That's what living like Jesus means sometimes.

For all of the difficulties I experienced in that house, there were so many valuable introductions made to me. Chicago is a bustling metropolis teaming with interesting characters. The diversity around me often invited me into powerful and vulnerable conversations with people I once would have thought of as strange and foreign. One evening, Madelyn brought me to a local church where an organization was hosting a discussion about race and privilege.

A dozen people sat in a circle on metal chairs in a sterile

church basement. The walls were cinder block, painted many times, likely the same high gloss white. A small table with a fresh pot of coffee, several small bottles of water and four or five bags of pretzels welcomed guests by the door. Everyone smiled warmly at each other and offered hushed greetings. Brief hugs were shared between a few, likely friends. Everyone in the circle seemed very different from the person next to them but the room felt united around the intention.

Discussion started tentatively. It wove in and out of other people's stories as we tried to imagine a path that might heal at least a little bit of the hurt caused by racism in the church. I tried to focus on the discussion but fought distraction. There were two men in the conversation who really captivated me.

Doug was in his mid twenties, thin and soft spoken. He was pursuing ordination at a nearby seminary. Single by choice, he professed he had never been attracted to women. He knew that he was gay, but chose to live a celibate life in sole pursuit of God. Steve was also gay, but didn't discover it until later in his life. He was older, made obvious by his long grey beard. He was much more boisterous than Doug, laughing heartily at times. It was only after he was married to a woman and raising a child was he able to admit his attractions. In an effort to live authentically they were divorcing, but she remained supportive even sitting by his side in the meeting.

These men, though I would never grow to know them any better than those meetings afforded, would change my life. Just the simple act of meeting them, and holding their gaze as they acknowledged their sexual identity lingered with me long after we parted ways.

For decades, I believed that homosexuality was wrong and people who practiced it were defective at best, and deviant at worst. I didn't think there were any such things as lesbians. They were just women who were broken and could be fixed if they made the effort. They just had bad fathers, or had been sexually abused or assaulted and felt it was safer to be with women. Gay men were just driven by insatiable lust and had shocked themselves into needing to have sex with one another because a normal sex life wasn't thrilling enough. I had no data to back up these beliefs, it just felt more logical than the existence of homosexuality. It doesn't work, therefore it must be bad. I looked into the eyes of those men, those gay Christian men, and felt love for them. Real genuine love and respect, not the pity or sickened self righteousness I felt before.

Something was knocked loose inside of me. My natural inclination after getting to know these men was to like them; to feel compassion for them and the struggles they faced. I wasn't interested in second guessing them, or admonishing them to do what I thought they should do. It seemed obvious to me that not only is that an easier strategy, but it's certainly kinder. And it assumes they are smart enough to figure out their own destiny and God was capable of changing their course if he wanted to. The balance of power in my heart shifted from self-righteousness to love.

It's still a debate whether I chose to explore scripture on the topic in order to restore myself to the "right path" of hating the sin, or to consider that perhaps I had missed something more important in the passages. Regardless of the guiding intention, I started devouring scriptures and scholarly writing on the subject. I was careful to consider the information from both sides of the discourse. Book after book, the more I read, the more I dug, the more and more lost I felt. It seemed that everyone was engaged in political rhetoric around the topic.

Wise, educated men and women stacked up on both sides. They couldn't even agree on what individual words meant, much less what behaviors those words were referencing. The division in the literature perfectly demonstrated what hundreds of years of the church fracturing itself into smaller and smaller denominations had long been pointing out: people will believe whatever the hell they want. The answer I sought was not in the arguments.

More than once, reading my Bible ended with it flying across the room and sliding down the opposite wall. I had a hard time talking to God during that time, though I kept trying. He struck me as an angry douche in the sky. Maybe I was an idiot for having bought this religion thing. Maybe there wasn't a God at all. I'd rather be a cosmic accident floating on a piece of dust in a random and chaotic universe than be forced to call another person an abomination. If what came naturally to them was such an awful thing, then the thing that created that nature, created them specifically to hate them. If everything taught to me held up, then some people were worthless. I was having a spiritual panic attack. It was less deconstruction, more implosion.

I missed Jesus. Jesus was kind. He played with kids. He fed masses of people. He let a whore wash his feet. He embraced lepers. He demonstrated with his life that his mission was to draw close to people. All people. He pointed to the trees and told us to be more like them, not worrying about what we would wear or eat. I wanted to be a tree. No one resents the natural way a tree grows in the forest. A tree doesn't have to second guess itself based on other trees. It just reaches.

Jesus was judgmental too. He had lots of behavioral boundaries that he would not tolerate people crossing. But none of them were about queer folk. He did mention Pharisees seventy-four times. He raged with violence against people who used religion to manipulate or destroy others. The entire twenty-third chapter of Matthew is an indictment of religious leaders prone to be led by their egos. There was a great deal of misinformation on how the Messiah changed things and Pharisees were always trying to take advantage and wield people's ignorance like a sword. Perhaps the religious elite were the ones fixing their crosshairs on the LGBT community. Queer people seemed to just be another scapegoat an insecure church could bully to feed her narcissism.

My search for answers changed course. There are lots of things that we face in modern society that weren't a thing in 25AD. Surely the God of the Universe, maker of all things, knew we'd face issues in the course of human development and would need a way to discern good from bad. How do we make judgments about fake news, AK-47s, nuclear weapons, genetic modification, universal healthcare, and whether or not you should put your prayer requests on Facebook? How could we know right from wrong?

Galatians 5: 19-23:

"The acts of the flesh are obvious: sexual immorality, impurity, and debauchery; idolatry, and witchcraft; hatred, discord, jealousy, fits of rage, selfish ambition, dissensions, factions and envy; drunkenness, orgies and the like. I warn you, as I did before, that those who live like this' will not inherit the kingdom of God.

But the fruit of the Spirit is love, joy, peace, patience, kindness, goodness, gentleness, faithfulness, and self-control. Against such things there is no law."

Those first couple of verses really knock the wind out of

you. There are at least eight of them that we all did on spring break. It's hard to fathom that doing these things, exempts you from heaven. Perhaps it's not about doing them, but rather basing one's whole life on them. Is it sexual immorality or impurity to not find men attractive? When I was young it was holy because it stopped me from the most profound impropriety: sex outside of marriage. Not wanting what I was allowed to want was good. Wanting what I was not allowed to want was bad. But denying what I wanted denies everything that could possibly grow from it. Gay people don't just run from orgy to orgy, they fall in love, they build lives together. For most couples sex encompasses only .005% of their lives. The rest of the time in their relationships they are discussing what's for dinner, and whose turn it is to take out the trash, LGBTQ people are no different in that respect. Does this one misalignment have to cost those people everything else?

There are a lot of things we ought not to be. Out of that list of 15, I had committed 13. You can decide which two I didn't. Odds are, I will commit them again in the future. So I guess I'm bad. But we don't learn to spot counterfeit money by looking at all the counterfeit money, we learn by looking at the real thing. What does a heart captivated by Jesus produce? If we want to know what is right, we look at its fruits. When this passage came alive to me, I had not admitted to myself, let alone anyone else, that I might be gay. I had only lived in denial and shame. As I looked around the landscape of my life I saw sadness, destruction, pain, self-hatred, fear, loneliness, and agony. It would have been an easy leap to say that these things existed because I was engaging in sinful behaviors. I spent a great deal of time in reflection over that very idea. What part of this life of mine was creating the turmoil? Was doing gay stuff screwing with my happiness? Was it the disobedience in this area that led to my destruction? Or was it hiding? Was it the denial? Was it self-loathing? Would God love me and bless my life if I learned how to be honest and speak the truth? Which is dearer to the heart of God, honesty or heterosexuality?

Brené Brown has been researching shame for years. In reading all of her groundbreaking work I saw myself unfolding in her words. She was right. Shame is the single most destructive force of my life. Shame is rooted in the notion that there is something fundamentally wrong with us. The church's ideology fueled that misguided belief in many of our hearts for decades. Could it be that the God of the Universe knows this without reading Brené Brown's work? Could it be that God wanted us to know that He knows we are fucked up? Could it be that Jesus' death was an attempt to wipe out the shame of the world in one grand gesture?

Imagine someone hiding in a dark closet whispering through a crack in the door to people they loved, "Dude, I'm gay," and hearing the reply, "Yeah, I know, get out here." The phrase would wipe the shame off of them like marks on a whiteboard. What if this whole Christian experience is us sitting in a closet whispering to God, "Dude, I'm (insert your point of shame here)" and him saying, "Yeah I know, get out here." What if the whole point of listing off all of these sins in long scary lists was God flinging open every person's closet and saying, "This is what people are made of. I am aware of it. I made a path away from the shame. None of you sucks harder than anyone else."

The modern church spends all of its time and money drawing sinners out of the shadows only to mutter, "Ew," when it sees them. Church shame, religious trauma, and Christian suicide are higher than ever, because the church is still insisting that the good news is that God can fix you and you too can live a charmed and prosperous life! If you just follow these rules you too can be enough and end your suffering! There is no place in the modern church to stand vulnerably *as you are* and feel the healing embrace of acceptance without hearing the humiliating whispers of judgment admonishing you to be someone else.

Several people I had met were gay and hid it. I knew how miserable and alone they were. They hated themselves so much, same as me. If I continued to deny what I really wanted and I subverted that truth as hard as I could, then every three or four years, the truth blistered out in a wild and reckless affair, what fruit would it produce? In countries where homosexuality is illegal and people are killed for it, are people better off? When parents condemn their kids for calling themselves gay, does love increase? Say, which fruit of the spirit is suicide? Which decision makes the most room for the fruit of the spirit to expand in my heart and bubble over into the lives of others? Acceptance or Condemnation?

Frustration burned in my gut. The situation felt like an ultimatum. Scholarship only deepened the gulf between the issues and I longed to choose a side and be done with it. The part of me that found great comfort in black and white clarity folded its arms in judgment against the part that wanted to put down my sword and love people.

The comfort of thinking I had a grasp on the truth was warm. It did inflate my self confidence to follow the rules and judge those incapable of the same devotion. If I let go of the rules, would I be abandoning God? Or would I just be abandoning the structure that made me feel safer? Was that structure making God bigger or smaller? Was my feeble human mind really capable of reducing God appropriately? Queer people existed, and there was a reason. Judgment created suffering, suffering was bad. Jesus hated the self righteous.

My conscience took three wide steps away from the rules and drew me deeper into the territory of the unknown. My whole heart could only say one thing with integrity: I don't know. For the first time, I began to understand the old colloquialism I had heard many times in church: I'm giving it to God. If he's the god of black and white rules, let him reign. If he's the god of love and compassion, so be it. Jennifer is made of compassion, acceptance and understanding. That is what she will be providing. He made me that way, and to Hell with him if he messed that up.

My run to Chicago was not a run toward a ministry, but rather a run away from a mess. It is very soothing to start fresh. Perhaps a large part of wanting to live there was longing for that clean slate. I wanted to talk about everything I was sorting through. I tried to talk to Madelyn but she shut me down. I wanted to tell her what I had been through and what I had been studying so I could work through all these swirling ideas, but she wasn't interested.

Over time, the memory of our friendship faded and it became harder to see the person I used to care about. There were so many ways she seemed to be keeping me at arm's length. I worried about what those reasons were. Maybe she resented me for the Taylor stink, maybe I creeped her out because of the old Croatia stuff, maybe I really was that bad at cleaning the toilet. I know that I wasn't altogether healthy during that chapter of my life. So many secret relationships had come and gone and I was quite a mess inside about them still. I knew she knew this about me too as she would relentlessly point out that she thought I was too sensitive, or too passive, or too anxious. She too had accumulated her own traumas and biases throughout her life. Her responses to me made me feel like a terribly invasive element in her universe. Longing to not be, regardless of what path I chose, it wasn't possible to avoid her anger or annoyance. Whether I was trying harder or trying less, I was trying wrong. She would start a conversation and I would feel attacked, but by the end of that conversation I was convinced I was the villain.

Three months had burned off of the calendar, my attention wrapped up in exegesis and research. I would make what effort I could in the house and accept that I was shit at all of it, expecting to be told I did it wrong. Taylor had to spend more and more time outside. It made him smell worse in general, but gave the house a chance to breathe. One day in early spring was journaling in my room and peaked out the window to see if he was still napping safely on the porch. I didn't immediately see him so I went outside to see what he was up to. The yard was big for a house in Chicago. Lined on all sides with a stone wall and iron gates it felt perfectly safe to leave him out there. The back gate was older and not the most secure but Taylor was lazy and wouldn't bother to escape.

I walked the perimeter of the yard and he was not there. He wasn't on the porch. He wasn't under the steps. He wasn't in the bushes. He wasn't inside. I called out as loud as I could.

"TAAAAAY LOOOOOR!"

"What are you doing?" muttered Madelyn.

"TAAAAAAYLOOOOOOOR!! I don't know where he is, I can't find him. TAAAAAAYLOOOOOOOR!!" My heart was starting to race.

"I'm sure he'll come home, don't worry about it."

"No, I need to find him. Maybe he slipped out the back gate, I'm just going to ride my bike around looking." I ran to unchain my bike.

"Where are you going to look?"

"I don't know, I just need to ride around and look everywhere, I don't know where he is. Just call me if he comes back."

I got on my bike and raced a block in each direction. He was short and fat, so it didn't seem like he could go far, but he was also a hound dog and if he caught an interesting scent he could be in Ohio before I noticed. I pedaled harder, trying not to think about him being somewhere hurt and scared. Up and down the streets surrounding my house I looked for him, occasionally calling out his name. My good sense was limited and I would have to catch myself occasionally before accidentally riding into traffic. The further I pedaled the further away from him I felt. I decided I would just go back to the house and pray that someone would find him and call the number on his tags.

I plopped down in the grass of the backyard, defeated. Madelyn came and sat next to me.

"I'm sure he'll be back. I'm sure he's fine," she said — her effort to comfort me.

"I hope so." The tears in my heart were making their way to my eyes, but I resisted.

She continued talking, offering solutions and conspiracies on his whereabouts. In the distance behind me I heard a whistle. Maybe it was a squeal. Was it someone's brakes? What was that? Then it struck me! The garage! I jumped to my feet and ran to the old garage in the very back of the yard. The door didn't shut all the way and as I pushed it open, sure enough, there was Taylor lying just inside the door, drool pooling beneath his face that was covered in dust. He figured out how to push his way in, but didn't have the thumbs to pull his way out.

I hugged him and squeezed him and gave him kisses and scratches. The tears I had been holding back in fear were flowing freely in relief. He gave me his focused attention as I scolded him for scaring me. Madelyn watched the whole scene and offered her perspective.

"You know, you might be too attached to Taylor."

A few weeks after she said that I told Madelyn I was going to leave. I gave her a lot of reasons. Taylor was too much. I wasn't making enough money to support myself. My brother needed my help with things. Those were all true. But I knew that moment with her in the yard offered me a kind of clarity I would not be able to shake off. All of the anxious hell I was internalizing, feeling so shitty for making her uncomfortable, tip-toe-ing through our lives to disrupt as little as I could and she couldn't hold in that stupid little judgment of me though I was weeping on the ground in joyous relief. Every disagreement we had after that would be haunted by that moment. Protecting me was not her job. She didn't care to connect with me. She wasn't interested in working things out if we disagreed. This was her ministry and her job was making a space for society's outcasts was her top priority. If the way she did it hurt me, then it wasn't meant for me.

It's not a bad strategy. When I think about her life up to that point, it makes sense. She's within her rights to walk through life that way. It was not the way I wanted to live. So after a total of six months in beautiful Chicago, packing up everything I brought and everything I had gained, I moved back home.

# 16

# Binding

Talking with Brandi illuminated a lot of patterns. It's difficult to reflect that much and not learn the rhythms of your own psyche. She helped me see the cycles I tended to keep and questioned how I might challenge myself to break them. Pleasing people seemed to be my dominant strategy for navigating relationships. If I could meet and maintain other people's expectations of me they would never turn against me, or hurt me. Other people's needs, feelings and perceptions were my main concern when making any decision. Being honest was a complicated strategy that could threaten people's love for me, so I avoided it. Brandi pointed out that pleasing others jeopardized my ability to hear my own feelings and see my own needs. It was a kind of self-abandonment. This was why my sexual identity was so distressing, why being the other woman was so devastating and why I continually felt like I couldn't share my experiences with anyone else. My needs were always an afterthought.

"Don't you ever want to just say, "Fuck it?" Brandi's eyebrows peeked out above her glasses.

"Yeah, that would be nice," I chuckled, "Fuck it."

"I mean, no offense, but people probably don't think about you as much as you think about what they might be thinking about you. What if you could just be yourself and it wouldn't be a big deal to others?"

"I'd probably love that."

"What could really happen if people really knew some of these truths about you?"

That question could have been minimizing, or it could have been investigative. The fact that I was deciding how to respond based on how I perceived her intentions pointed back to the problem she had just illustrated. Even in trying to answer her therapeutic question I was more worried about what she wanted than what was true for me. The truth for me was, yes, most people in the world didn't care about who I had slept with or what I was doing with my life. But there were very clear and distinct ways that being gay could destroy my life that Brandi didn't understand. For example, I could be fired from my job.

When I returned home from Illinois, I was badly in need of work. I had to pay my brother rent and I had to find a new car as I had sold mine to survive the Chicago winter. My marketable skills fell into two categories, telecommunications, and Christian ministry. There was only one cable company nearby and despite getting a second interview I wasn't offered a job. I don't blame them as I couldn't have been less passionate about getting back into that business. I had left the corporate world for a life with more substance and meaning and I still wanted that. I couldn't picture that being outside of ministry, so I just went for it.

I applied to every available ministry job I could find. I got an interview at a thrift store, and was immediately turned away for being overqualified, but they passed my information to a boys' shelter. They had work that was more up my alley, they said. I interviewed and was offered a job right away. I got the impression that they weren't interviewing me as much as they were trying to convince me that I should work for them. It seemed like the employees worked there because they were called to it, not for the lovely experience, or the livable wage. When I showed up to accept the offer, I was given a tax form, a demographics sheet, and a lifestyle agreement.

Perhaps you have never heard of a lifestyle agreement. Maybe you have never had the joy of working for a place that paid close attention to your spiritual life and the details of how you practiced that faith. This wasn't new to me. In college there was a lifestyle agreement. Volunteering as a counselor at church camp came with a lifestyle agreement. Signing up for a year of mission work required signing a lifestyle agreement. Most ministries exist to further the message of the church body that funds them. It's necessary to have everyone employed there be committed to the exact same mission and live out that mission in the exact same way. You have to have a legal path to let people go if they reflect poorly on the message. If they sign a piece of paper committing to the ministries values then that ministry can cut them loose for any number of private behaviors.

Most of the principles in the document in front of me were a no-brainer. "Employees affirm that Jesus Christ is the Son of God. Employees commit to live in such a way as to promote the principles of Christianity including the avoidance of illegal activity and public drunkenness. Employees will commit to membership in a local church and attend services regularly.

Employees commit to maintain pure and Godly relationships. This includes not engaging in sexual behaviors outside the context of marriage, extra-marital affairs, or homosexual relationships."

This was religious freedom. This is what they would use to punish me if I fell in love with a girl. This was the clause that got my first love kicked out of Croatia. Fucking clause. I was mad to see it. But was this the first time this agreement pissed me off? All of my other ministerial opportunities came with agreements. Before this one, they felt like a simple safeguard. If my employer could fire me for public drunkenness, then I would never so much as sniff alcohol for fear of going broke! It had been easy to be black and white. I had found a sense of safety in someone else's authority over me. Now it seemed stifling and overreaching. How does an employer find the audacity to dictate how I spend my life outside of work? But I was cornered. Between being broke and longing to impact the world with faith, it seemed I would have no other choice. If I wanted to have a job that mattered to me, it meant signing off on my human right to grow as I saw fit. I had to grow as they saw fit. I signed it. I didn't have a girlfriend. I was dating boys. I was pretty certain I would not be sleeping with any of those. It's not right of them to force me to do this. But it's not wrong. It's just politics. I wasn't a sellout. This was business.

For a while, the job was worth it. I worked on and off during the week and at night. I spent mornings telling young men to clean their rooms and evenings listening to painful stories of parental abandonment. I would wake them up every Sunday and push them out the door to church. I would lead devotions with them every night and hammer home the importance of living a life like Jesus. This was it. I was being a missionary to these boys, and I was serving a higher calling. I was making a difference. I was cultivating a passion for serving un-housed teenagers. I wasn't doing anything bad or wrong anymore. I was fully committed to my faith and ministry.

Sometimes, the work was hard and created a spiritual dissonance in me. We would have weekly meetings to talk about all of the residents and their progress in school and toward jobs. Sometimes those veered off into subject areas that made me feel uncomfortable. If a boy seemed a little gay, he would get watched closer. If he were Muslim, we would have to discuss how and where he could practice his faith. There would be celebrations if a kid told us he had abandoned his old religion to trust in Jesus. That didn't feel as good as I imagined it would.

There was a tiny office in the boys home that regular staff could sit in to write notes and make phone calls. I was there one evening when a young man came in and sat down. The room was sparsely decorated with just an old metal desk, a bookshelf and two armchairs.

"Miss Jennifer, can I ask you a question?" Shawn was 19. His skin was a flawless dark brown. His hair cut close with a tight fade. When he smiled he used his whole body and he could spend hours playing racing video games.

"Sure honey, come sit with me." I used pet names often. Partly because boys came and went and misnaming them was embarrassing for me and hurtful to them. But mostly because there weren't many women in their lives who spoke to them affectionately. It felt tender to call them nice things.

"Do you think my Mom is in Hell?" Gut-punched by his question I gasped for breath, unsure how to answer. I looked over at him trying to discern what was happening inside of him. He sat calmly on the edge of the chair, his hands stuffed into his sweatshirt pockets. His eyes were serious.

"What? Shawn what do you mean, why would you ask such a question?"

"I'm serious, Miss Jennifer, today at church the preacher talked about how if you die and you aren't a Christian, you go to hell," his eyes were getting wetter, "My mom was a good lady, but she never went to church. I don't remember much about her anymore, but I don't think she was a Christian, so that means she's in hell, don't it?"

Stalling for time, I got up from my chair and crouched in front of him clasping his hands in mine.

"Shawn, buddy." I sighed a heavy cleansing breath and glimpsed up at the open door. I didn't want any coworkers to hear me say this. "Only God knows what's in someone's heart. I don't know your Mom, but God does. He knows what a good lady she was. If she belongs in Heaven, then that's where she is. Hell isn't for good ladies."

To an Evangelical, to a part of myself, to my boss, that was heresy. It was theologically wrong. But his question hit me right at the intersection of all of my doubts. My compassion for his grieving heart was bigger than my passion for dogma. I was glad he chose to ask me. Another staff might have hemmed and hawed and let this child think his mother was burning in hell.

Shawn was one of many young men who illustrated for me how wide the gulf was between our lives. Who was I to tell these boys anything? I couldn't minister to their souls. My life was a thousand miles away from theirs. They needed a kind of help I wasn't equipped to give them. I wasn't even smart enough to know what it was. Investing in them spiritually should have been an afterthought to the help they actually needed. They needed food, beds, skills, and jobs. We were requiring them to stop sagging their pants, go to church, and say their prayers in order to sit at our table. It felt manipulative to trade their obedience for shelter.

I found myself in the same space I had been before. I had grown up thinking I wanted to serve others from the overflow of my spirit. I had tried so many paths, but once I got inside a "ministry" they all left me feeling sick. They all felt manipulative. I'll give you this ticket to heaven if you sacrifice your culture, heritage, and identity. I'll feed lots of people, but let's post it online for clout. I'll let you sleep in this house for free, but you have to say you love Jesus. Was ministry really about loving others? Or was it only about convincing people to be Team Jesus. If whatever you were giving or selling or swapping didn't recruit bigger numbers or bigger donors, would it still be worth doing? Would I find this discontent at the bottom of everything we called 'ministry'? Is there any possible path that is based solely on helping other people without agenda or manipulation?

It seemed weird that I would sign my life away for this kind of work. Even more strange that I willingly lived a duplicitous life in fear of losing such a job. But it was a paycheck, and I did love those boys. So it was a big enough fear to keep me quiet.

Clearly, being openly gay was a threat to my employment, but it wasn't the only threat. Anyone who grew up as addicted to christian contemporary music as I had was tuned into the carnage of Jennifer Knapp's punishing return to the spotlight. She had not only come back to us, she had come out to us. My old gossiping church band buddy had been right. She was gay. I couldn't have cared less and it didn't change anything

I felt about her, her music, or her faith. I loved her, gay or straight. It did, however, motivate me to spend nights lying in my bed, re-listening to her catalog. Her sexuality reincarnated her music into an entirely different creature. All the pleading, all the longing, all the feeling unworthy and not enough, it all made so much sense in the light of gay.

She was quite a trooper over the next several months. All over the media, Christian magazines, blogs, and even CNN wanted to talk with the great fallen CCM star. She took it on with such courage. People famous for denouncing homosexuality (some after being caught in it) came after her like bloodthirsty, snarling wolves. Is this how it goes for every Christian who tries to come out? Do all the high-ranking authorities in our microcosms come out and try to beat us back in the closet? They lunged at her, snapped at her, and attempted to drag her back into the closet, but for the most part she sat calmly, peacefully, and contentedly gay. She seemed wide awake and completely settled while her opposition flailed in delirium. Man, what I could do with her vibe.

Eventually the hype around her faded. The wolves could see they couldn't beat her and withdrew to fight against some other sad sheep gone astray. She went back to the business of writing beautiful music and playing it for people who stayed to hear it. It was so encouraging to my heart to watch her be so brave. Unfortunately, watching the wolves come for her resolved me to keep looking for the one man that I could tolerate. I couldn't tell you which fruit of the Spirit the wolves were demonstrating, if any. But I was sure I didn't want to be at the snout end of those sharp teeth.

Point being, I knew the enemies I was facing. For decades, seated with them at their round tables during their discussions of war. I intimately knew who they hated and how passionately so. Despite Brandi's encouragement toward authenticity it still felt like too much risk. If there was a shred of hope for me, it could be found in only one place: the arms of a man.

# 17

# Interesting

Graduate school is supposed to be hard, and it was. Surprisingly, it was hard for reasons far different from the ones I had anticipated. I expected I would be challenged academically, and was afraid I wouldn't be able to keep up with the workload. I didn't expect to explore myself so deeply. No one warned me that I might go through the levels of inner conflict that I was experiencing. At no point in my education was that struggle more obvious than in my fourth semester.

Despite struggling to understand my thoughts about God, faith and sexuality, I fully recognized that my views shaped how I treated myself and others. All my years in ministry had carved deep ruts of "helpful strategies" that I would dispense when someone asked me for help. The kind of advice I was used to giving often pointed people toward the church's understanding of good behavior. Though I was far from ironing out my beliefs, I recognized the important role my faith was going to play in doing therapy. There were strong ethical standards against forcing your own beliefs on your clients and I wondered how I might help someone if I genuinely thought that what they were doing was wrong. How do I not just tell them about the better path? How do I incorporate my beliefs into my helping without hurting anyone? Once I figured out my doubts I'd probably still be a Christian and thereby I needed to know how to be a Christian Counselor. "Spiritual Issues and Marriage and Family Therapy" was an elective available the next fall. It was taught by one of the program's founding faculty who, as I understood it, also had his Masters of Divinity. That seemed like an answered prayer.

Very unfortunately, weeks before the class was scheduled to start, our beloved professor suffered a stroke that prevented him from teaching. I hadn't met the person who would replace him, but I felt sure they would be a disappointment. Her name was Julie. I was very skeptical. I had never heard of this lady before. She was an adjunct professor, and I hadn't yet taken anything she taught. The only gossip I could get off the street was that she was "interesting." Interesting? What does that mean?

As I walked into the classroom, Julie stood leaning against the desk at the front of the room. Her feet were crossed casually and she folded her arms surveying the small flock of students as they chatted and got settled. She smiled at me with a warm sincerity as I found a place among the group. At first glance, she seemed normal enough, she wore sandals and leggings with a flowing colorful blouse. She was older than me, but not by much. Her jewelry was unique, symbolic certainly, but the symbols were for ideologies that weren't familiar to me.

As she opened the class, she seemed nervous. She apologized that we weren't going to have the original professor. Struck by his sudden illness, she held back emotion discussing it. She vowed to do her best and asked for our understanding as she would be only a few steps ahead of us in some of the materials.

The disappointment came quickly as I surveyed the syllabus. I was way off in my understanding of the objectives of the class. It wasn't at all about being a Christian counselor, but rather a way to explore lots of "other-than-Christian" beliefs so that we might be able to help anyone we saw utilize any faith they had to find hope and resilience. We were going to spend a lot of time discovering all kinds of faiths other than our own. I understood the need, but I couldn't hold back the sighs.

There were other Evangelical students in the classroom, likely having expected the same material and feeling the same disappointment. As they voiced their complaints, I could hear my own heart but also felt a desire deep within me pulling me in another direction. After all I had been through, I had hidden in the corner of my heart the desire for God to be bigger than all of the rhetoric. Maybe Julie could show me something I truly longed for. I pushed my disappointment to the side and opened my mind to the content.

As it would turn out, I really liked Julie. The masses were right about her, interesting was the perfect word. She was warm and funny and seemed at home in herself even though she wasn't entirely like everyone else. I felt connected to her in a way that I couldn't put my finger on. It was a familiar connection, though I couldn't discern what it was exactly. Because of all that I had been through, that scared me.

I listened to her speak and felt aligned. Was she a kindred spirit like Rosina? Someone would say something in class that was childish or dirty, and we would catch each other in a devilish grin. Did I have a crush on her like Heather? She stood in defense of me when I would try to be self-deprecating. Was she mothering me? When I was obviously struggling or making something wildly complicated, she would step in with a thought that would simplify everything. It was soothing, and maddening. She had a higher perspective on lots of things. Maybe she was the pastor I never truly got to lean on. She knew things. I don't mean she was smart or wise, although I do think she is. I mean, it seemed she knew *me*, specifically. She would look at me as though she were reading my mind and it didn't freak me out.

The truth I didn't know then and that maybe escapes you now was that Julie was a therapist doing what a therapist does. She believed in me. She made space for me. She defended me against myself. I know these skills. Julie and professors like her taught me these skills. I use these skills with countless other people every single day. It was what we in the biz call 'unconditional positive regard.' and Julie was a master of it. Basically, regardless of what I thought, what I felt, and what I did, I was a valuable human being. In Julie's simple therapeutic approach to just accept and value me as I was, the big, heavy weight of living up to someone else's ideal came crashing to the floor.

At first, that's scary. If we can't discern someone's motivations, we can't please them. So we spend time projecting other relationships onto them. We try to categorize the relationship, test-driving theories about them through our experiences, believing that knowing their motivations will protect us. Then we stop resisting and allow their positive regard to saturate our hearts. They believe in us, and eventually we join them. When I could just accept Julie's faith in me, my core could relax with belief in myself. Her posture toward me communicated, "You're trustworthy to figure this out." When it came to the path ahead, whether it was related to God, or work, or my own identity; no matter what I discovered, or what happened next, I felt in my bones I was going to be okay.

Each week in class we would talk about a new way of thinking. We were reading books that reframed the story of Jesus in different ways, interesting ways. It was fun to explore new ideas about a man with whom I had grown too familiar.

"In your reading this week, the author talked about the narrow path. Traditional Christianity views that as being an absolute, rule based path that everyone must find and walk. But here we are looking at the narrow path as more of your own individual journey, more authenticity than structure. What did you think?"

"I loved that idea." said the girl next to me, "Finding your own way can be so hard and this affirms that."

"It's a nice thought, but I'd rather believe the Bible. The narrow way is narrow because there is a right way to live, it's about doing what God said to do," argued Bethany from across the room. Bethany was a very expressive evangelical. Her hair was perfect, her make-up always applied just-so. She spoke often of how she had waited to have sex until she was married, and how blessed she was to have met her Godly husband. She was nice. But we weren't friends.

"Okay, good thoughts, anyone else?" Julie moved on with grace.

"I felt kind of relieved reading it," I said. "I felt like Bethany for a long time, but something about this felt like it gave me permission to trust myself." Julie smiled and nodded.

"It's a perfectly nice theory, but precarious." said Edward. He was a good guy. He wore intellect like a personality type, and often spoke using four syllable words. I remember being intimidated by him early on for his use of perseverate. But I grew to discover he was just nerdy like that. He was raised in the Church of Jesus Christ of Latter Day Saints and I loved talking with him at parties. Him with his scholarly Mormon thoughts and I with my Evangelical Bible degree, could sit for hours comparing doctrine and taking turns admiring one another's faith. He wasn't even enrolled in this class, but Julie let him sit in. "Scripture is littered with instruction and the verses surrounding those about the narrow path point to many of those rules. It seems theologically irresponsible to hypothesize such a meaning."

"Okay, I hear that." said Julie. She was good at never coming out with her own concrete opinion on any topic. She was not a propagandist or antagonist. She was just clearing the space.

Watching all of the different people talk and have different opinions offered me a very unique perspective. It was as though all of my different parts were in a room having a conversation. Bethany was my inner terrified Evangelical. Edward, my intellect. And I was free to embody my curiosity without the fear that I would get lost for too long without one of them stepping in to remind me of "God's perspective."

Julie continued parading unique perspectives in front of us. We met a Druid who taught us about trees, a pagan who taught us about our guardians, a Baha'i who shared her thoughts on the oneness of faiths, and a Unitarian who talked about universal truths. We visited a rabbi in a temple, an Imam in his mosque and our own spirit guides in the forests of our own subconscious.

The journey eventually started triangulating me between Bethany and Edward. My anger crystalized at their discomfort that had become emblematic of the patriarchy's control over me. Were leaders I thought wise really scared of rose quartz and incense? Were such things a pathway to demonic possession or were they just afraid of what would happen should we all learn how to think for ourselves and connect to the wild heart beating inside of us? Anger spilled out in discussions with my classmates, but the war was really raging inside of me between parts of myself.

It wasn't easy sorting through those old scripts. The church had spent a great deal of effort convincing me, convincing all of us, that we (the believers) were not to be trusted. Flesh was me. Spirit was God. The message of the Spirit never changed. His will was written, in black and white (and sometimes red), plain as day. Our responsibility as followers was to always do what was in line with the Spirit and crucify our flesh. Our instinct, our intuition, our vibes, our knowing, our third eye, our empathy, our longings, our needs, our wishes, our desires—all flesh. Not just fallible, but always bent toward evil. Hammered into us, week after week, was a deep abiding suspicion of our every inner groaning. The expectation was that we would completely empty ourselves of self and allow Jesus (whom we had murdered) to carry out his will through us. We were bought at a price, and we owed on that debt.

Truthfully, Evangelicals used their instincts all the time, but you weren't allowed to call it your instinct. You had to call it the Spirit. "I felt God moving in my spirit to give that man $5." "I could feel the Lord telling me that man was no good and I needed to stay clear." The Spirit could tell you something that didn't make any sense otherwise and you had to do it no matter how much you didn't want to. Conversely, no matter your desires, unless God says it's okay and you can confirm it with Scripture, you're wrong.

In that class with Julie, as I was hearing people reveal

connections with ancestors and past lives or the healing aspects of nature, my heart would smile with a knowing, but my "Spirit" would quickly condemn me. I was experiencing an internal divorce, and was scared neither parent would want me when papers were signed.

# 18

# The High Priestess

One late September evening, Julie came in and announced that the special guest she had planned was unable to join us. We were going to have to settle for her lecture on the evening's material. As she spoke, she rifled through a large bag. She placed a velvety little pouch cinched tightly at one end in front of every other student. Both of my neighbors received the special package and so I was left to peer over their shoulders as they revealed what was inside.

"Today's lesson is about Tarot. What do we know about Tarot?"

The neighbor to my left gently removed a deck of cards from her pouch and separated them carefully, examining each one. Every card revealed a new colorful drawing of people and animals engaged in various activities. To my right were very different looking cards, darker, more mystical in nature. The figures on them were human-like, but not entirely. They were angels and fairies and other-worldly.

Bethany scooted her cards to her neighbor, unwilling to engage with them directly as she spoke. "These are fortune teller cards." Her ignorant southern drawl amplified her disdain, but highlighted the fears hiding deep in my own chest. These were objectively witchcraft to people from my world.

"Some people use them for that, sure, Bethany. But really Tarot is just a tool that people use to communicate with the spiritual world. Sometimes it's connecting to God, Angels or Spirit guides, and sometimes it's communicating with ourselves and our deeper consciousness."

We all sat quietly examining the different decks and passing them between us, unsure of what questions to ask about them.

"Does anyone use these as a part of their own spiritual practice?" One hand raised and then shrunk into the gesture for so/so.

"Would anyone like to try it?"

A few hands shot up and she quickly set up one of the spare tables so everyone could watch. She sat across from the first student swirling cards in front of her, mixing them all around. "Do you have a question to ask? Or a particular topic that needs some clarity?"

"Sure, um…how about my family?"

Julie continued swirling until she felt satisfied with the shuffle. Then she offered the deck to the student to cut. After that she plucked three cards, one at a time from the top of the deck and placed them face down on the table.

"We're going to ask for information on the past, present and future of your family, okay? The first card represents the past." She flipped the card and it made a snap as she placed it down. "The Star. Just take a moment and look at the card and tell me what you think or feel."

"It looks happy. It looks free."

"Good," said Julie, "This card does represent hope, contentment. It means everything is peaceful, all needs are met." She lifted the second card, "This one is about the present. It's the five of swords. What do you see?"

"It looks like there was just some sort of fight, and two guys are walking away sad."

"Yea, this one can represent loss or difficulty." My classmate sat pensively as the rest of us held our breath for her. "The third one is for the future: The four of wands."

"That looks happy, like a party, maybe a wedding. Definitely a celebration."

"Yes, this one symbolizes celebration, everything coming together." They both sat staring at the three cards. "I won't make you share anything personal, but do these cards speak to you about your family?"

"Yes" she whispered, her voice cracking with emotion.

That was it? I was so intrigued. I wanted to be next, but it would take three or four more people before I found the courage to admit it. Julie was preparing to put things away. Some students had started checking phones and wandering away, starting to lose interest.

"Before you put it away, can I do it?" I asked.

"Sure, do you have a specific question?"

"Can we just say I have a general wondering?"

She laughed, "Sure, but isn't there *anything* you'd like to ask about specifically? It's just more interesting that way." Her follow up question alerted me to the fact that I had written this woman at least a half dozen deeply personal papers about my complicated spiritual life.

"Oh. Well sure, how about…I dunno…love," I said, trying hard to be casual despite having spent the last hour longing to hear what the cards had to say about my love life.

"Okay, love," she chuckled. I sat back and watched as her hands danced around the table pushing the cards forward and backward, swirling and twirling them between us. She scooped them all up and tidied the pile then placed the deck in front of me. I drew a cleansing breath to sanctify the moment before reaching out and cutting them.

She pulled the cards from the top of the deck and placed them softly in front of me. "You know the drill right?"

"Yes ma'am."

"For the past you have the ten of swords. Tell me what you see."

"Umm, geez. I see a guy laying dead under a black sky with ten swords in his back!" My heart raced. What a grizzly sight.

She smiled tenderly, "Okay. This card can represent defeat, loss, suffering."

I grimaced at the thought of learning more horrifying truths. She turned over the next card. "Your present is the Hermit."

"Ha. okay, a lonely sad old man."

"It could be, it also means retreat, introspection, wisdom in isolation."

"I guess that's better. But I hope my future card is a little better."

She smiled and turned over the last card. "The High Priestess."

"Looks like some kind of religious leader, a holy lady?"

"She's wise. She represents maturity and trusting one's own intuition. She sits between the dark and the light. There's a complexity, a duality."

"So I need to trust myself and I'll be okay?"

"Maybe. What they inspire is really up to you."

She knew I wanted to be told what to do and was refusing.

She knew my problem was that I had been told what to do for too long and it had severed my relationship with myself, with my own intuition. Or, she didn't know any of that and I was putting it on her because I wanted to hear it from someone I trusted, and I genuinely didn't trust me. Now Tarot was insinuating that I maybe should. I sensed that the activity was going to have a profound effect on me, and was genuinely afraid that effect was going to be demonic somehow. My inner Evangelical watched and waited for me to burst into flames, but the whole thing was no more innocuous than Gideon laying out a fleece in the book of Judges. I wanted so much to trust myself. Was the devil hijacking me through Tarot to soothe me into listening to my flesh? Or had Tarot just provoked my deeper wisdom to guide me toward healthy self-esteem?

Once she dismissed us I walked out slowly and headed to my car. It wasn't an unusual occurrence for me to sit for a long time in the parking lot after that class. My mind, normally busy with anxiety or fantasy, sat quietly with me, listening to the ringing in my ears. I watched my classmates file out of the building, laughing and talking. They weren't fazed by the activity. Why was I? I tilted my head back to lean on the headrest and closed my eyes counting the length of each breath.

In the New Testament, when Jesus died, the Earth shook and the veil to the inner sanctuary was torn. As I sat there contemplating the events of the evening, I was reminded of that moment in scripture. Before then, only the ritually sanctified men of a particular tribe were allowed to enter, allowed to experience the full radiance of God. After the veil tore, everyone could enter the holiest of holy places.

We had spent that whole semester learning about all of the various ways different people accessed the holy places in their lives. What are we really longing to find in that place? If someone were truly in a sacred space staring God (or the great whomever) in the face, what would they do? What would you do? What would I do? It's a rhetorical question, you're reading a book, I already know what I would do.

If I were standing before God in whatever shape He or She or They took, I would ask one question. My entire life points toward it. Everything I do; everything I think or say; every goal I chase; every pursuit I decline; every day dream that captures my imagination; every prayer I've written; song I've sung; every joke, every lie, every confession; every religious, sexual, physical or emotional experience I've ever had begs one question.

Am I enough?

Am I ever enough? Am I pretty enough, smart enough, cool enough, sexy enough, happy enough, doing enough, holy enough, safe enough, wild enough? The question lingers underneath and around everything like a foul stench from a dead animal you can't locate. If I'm not enough, then I'm never going to make it. I'm never going to feel okay. I'll just keep ruining everything.

That brief Tarot reading not only highlighted that lifelong fear but soothed it with a response: trust your intuition. Trusting myself is all I have ever wanted; to stop feeling like a 12 year old stuck inside an adult suit. It struck me like an axe to the back that my childhood faith had suspended me in self-doubt like a body part in formaldehyde. The Evangelical cure to my insecurity had always been to affirm it. If you feel like shit, it's because you are. Everything I touched turned to shit. That's why Jesus had to die. A holy God can't chill with a skank. You're right, you're not enough. You'll *never* be enough.

Maybe Evangelical Christianity was some bullshit.

My hands clapped over my ears to block out the sound of my own thoughts. Trolling around with other religions was all fine and dandy, but that right there was straight up heresy. "This is because you touched Tarot cards, Jennifer! It's divination! You've poisoned your mind!" The presence of the voice of condemnation in my head both annoyed me and soothed me that I had not lost my faith altogether. Thinking the thoughts terrified me that I was on another slippery slope that was going to result in me crawling out of the rubble of another disastrous attempt at living a happy life.

Though I felt a deep and scary insecurity watching some of the walls of my faith crumbling around me, I knew I couldn't put the bricks back either. They no longer made any sense. Why would the God who created me leverage inner criticism and self-condemnation to keep me afraid of failing? Why would the God of all things be so threatened by ideas? How did it destroy the kingdom for me to acquire the belief that I'm no better or worse than anyone else? Did I want to be a part of that kind of kingdom? God wasn't disintegrating in front of me, just a particular image of God. At my deepest level, I still sensed that God was both real and powerful and I wanted to be freed from the dogma that separated us. I longed to find myself, find God and love us both. Could I believe in him and also believe in myself? He needed to answer these questions. I needed a touch or a comfort or a sign that only I could interpret that was undeniable.

This wasn't the same as those old made-up signs I "prayed for" back in the day. "Dear Lord, if you want me to be a missionary, let them run out of milk in the cafeteria tonight." They *always* ran out of milk in the cafeteria. I knew what I wanted and was setting God up like a toddler at tee ball. No, no, I needed the real deal.

I punched on the overhead light and groped around in my bag for my journal. I felt lost. I had no idea where I was headed. Writing prayers always helped. Maybe I could organize my thoughts and feel better. Maybe I could remind myself of the truths that seemed to be slipping away.

"No." I said aloud. I tossed my journal against the window.

# 19

# Wishes

The shifter let out a thud as a put my car in gear. Silence filled the air as my headlights sliced through the dark night on the long country roads back to my brother's house. A burning tinge of envy seared into my heart as I reflected on all of the guests we had met during class. They sung so confidently of their loving God and his care for them. Their spirits were lifted by their faith and brought them a feeling of wholeness. Mine had done the same in the beginning. Immediately after we were advised that we were fallen and hopeless sinners, hero Jesus ran in and offered us his hope. What a bargain. What a deal. What a relief.

Jesus saw my ugliness and called me to him anyway. The first dose of Jesus' love was healing, unconditional, unearned. My ugliness, though. Where did that come from? My parents never told me I was bad. Despite the absolute emotional violence of elementary school and middle school, classmates never told me I was ugly. No one in 35 years had ever actually looked me in the face and told me I was not enough.

There are people in this world not so lucky. There are

terrible parents out there who shame their children and sear their hearts with hateful things. Children suffer tremendous abuse. But I hadn't.

Yes, like everyone else I had endlessly compared myself to other people, a common side effect of growing up in a capitalist society. Every 15 minutes there's a new commercial showing me a product that could make me better, or make my life easier. Corporations benefited when I felt inferior to someone else. But even ruthless corporations never directly said, "You are disgusting." No one ever had. No one except for the church, that is.

Only in Sunday service, Wednesday Bible study and Thursday small groups through the voices of pastors, teachers, deacons, and elders would actual human beings call me deplorable, disgusting, or an abomination. They didn't even bother to feign a sheepishness, or tenderness. It was full-throated with their chests confidently puffed. I was ashamed, because the church spent 25 years actively shaming me. It struck me for the first time that all of those years of hearing the church shame and condemn me, combined with my own voice wailing in song about my own wickedness and wretchedness had indeed been abusive.

The church was the body that handed down all of the rules and standards that I continually failed to meet. Some of them seemed completely materialized out of thin air, not directly out of scriptural teachings. Certainly, four years of studying the Bible in my Evangelical university doesn't make me a Biblical scholar, but the path between Biblical writings and Evangelical doctrine is a wildly indirect path that I was certainly never able to fully track. Maybe if I had been a better student back then and worked harder to understand how we got from there to here, I'd be less lost now. Lost was a good word for this feeling. God wasn't the problem. The Bible wasn't the problem. Even I wasn't the problem. The man-made, politically poisoned, money obsessed, size obsessed, success obsessed, power hungry, wildly misguided church was the problem.

The gravel crunched beneath my tires as I pulled into my brother's driveway. My parent's modest old home stood dark on the nearest hill. The familiarity of that farm washed over me and I felt safety surrounding me. Home is such a warm and comforting place. That's all I longed to feel with God: home. By teaching me to doubt my intuition, church had robbed me of having a home inside myself. By teaching me of God's wrath, they robbed me of a home in the universe, in the greater plan. They stole my belonging from all things and held it hostage until I could perform as they saw fit. And I never performed as they saw fit.

I walked out into the field that separated us and picked a spot on the grass to lie down. Late September was pushing a faint chill into the dense southern air. I felt the itch of the grass tickle my arms and wondered briefly about how many bugs I was crushing.

The blackness above me was deep and limitless. Stars sparkled vague reminders of my insignificance. The sound of my racing inner dialogue hushed to listen to the gentle whir of crickets. Fresh air burned my nostrils as I drew slow cleansing breaths. My hands rested on my chest feeling the rise and fall of my anxiety as it calmed inside of me.

Still on my back, I turned to watch the rising moon ascend the distant hill. A blurred object blocked my view, and I pulled back my head to bring it to focus. It was a dainty little seeding dandelion. Its wild fluffy mane fanned out from its core inviting my inner 6-year-old out to play. I sat up, plucked it from the ground and held it in front of me as I examined it. Its delicate shape sang to me memories of childhood summers. Hours I could spend delightfully wishing, infuriating the neighbors as I blew weed seeds all over their lawns. They weren't weeds at all to me. They were beautiful. Not only that, but they were magical! With a single puff of breath it released dozens of tiny flecks of magic dust into the universe to manifest my wildest fantasies.

What would I wish if there were magic in this old flower? Love? Yes. Riches? Maybe. Deeper still, I knew what I longed for from my bones was a peace – a confidence. I wanted to feel I belonged here and that I was capable of more than creating messes. I wanted to find my way. With my eyes pinched tightly closed, I blew its seeds into the darkness.

I rose from the ground and brushed the grass and dirt from my clothes. Hungry mosquitoes had found the buffet of my skin and I needed to take the existential crisis indoors. I traded my jeans and sweatshirt for a tank top and pajama pants and eased myself into bed. Pulling a tattered quilt over my cool skin, I rested my head in my hand and tugged the ribbon marking my place in my journal. I looked at the blank pages and longed for them to soothe me the way they once had. I pondered what might help.

What I knew for sure was that I couldn't keep up the performance my spirituality had become. Belief isn't something you can fake and I had been faking for a very long time. Whatever the church was selling, I just wasn't buying it. But I was still scared. I didn't want to go alone and I did at least believe that someone made me to be me. This whole experience of life with it's wildness, the complexities of our thoughts and the intensities of our connections tell me that it's significant. This journey is not for nothing. I wanted whomever was authoring this production to draw me near and show me just how incredible it was.

I picked up my pen and wrote the prayer I could feel with my whole body.

*"This is what I'm asking of you, God. It's just me and you here. I don't want the world's words. I don't want mediocre half-ass culture. I don't want Christianity, or Baptistisms, or colloquialisms, or fluff. I'm not afraid of metaphysical, mystical, or odd beliefs. What I am afraid of is that I'm the reason my life sucks. I'm also afraid you aren't real at all. I need your help. I will go any way you lead, but it has to be your unique words spoken directly to my unique heart that guide me. I will be honest, but you have to lead me. I need a real response."*

# 20

# Signs

Like a radio dial set to a particular station, I was tuned in. Squished into the second-hand leather couch at the boys shelter, I scribbled the word "Respond" in different fonts and sizes on the page in front of me. Something had happened the night before. My honest prayer to God, multiplied by a wish on a dandelion had combined with the enormity of my desperation to shift the whole planet. Heaven and Earth heard me, and I knew it. All my receptors were turned up to their highest sensitivities so I would not miss God's response. He was free to encourage me forward into freedom, or he had all the opportunity to condemn me in his righteousness and stricken me with illness. I was willing to hear whatever he sent.

The TV was on low, so it wouldn't distract the guys from getting ready. Boys poured in one by one and waited for each other. One young man asked me if he could change it to a church service and I allowed it. The preacher on the screen had already hit the fever pitch of his sermon.

His face was red and the veins in his neck throbbed as he

shouted. "GOD CAN DO IT-ah! DON'T. THINK. THAT GOD… CAN'T. DO IT-ah! IF YOU HAVE FAITH-ah, SMALL AS A MUSTARD SEED ah. GOD-WILL-GIVE-YOU WHAT-YOU ASK-HIM-FOR-ah."

"Brothers and sisters-ah," he said quietly, "I believe that the next 90 days are going to change your life. I believe God has blessings on the way and you can expect him to deliver in 90 days. Can I get an Amen!? Can I get a hallelujah?! DO YOU WANT YOUR 90 DAYS OF BLESSINGS FROM GOD!? JUST SAY "GOD, I BELIEVE IN YOUR 90 DAYS! I NEED YOUR 90 DAYS, I CLAIM YOUR 90…"

The screen went black, "Let's go guys," I called out, placing the remote on the table.

My own pastor's message danced right past my ears at church. I was thinking about the preacher on TV. After last night, my eyes felt opened. Everything seemed staged, performed, as manipulative as a cheese-y movie on an obscure cable TV channel. That stupid preacher on TV just whipping himself up into a stroke inducing frenzy, no doubt just moments from telling people they needed to send him money. 90 days. What a fucking joke.

Wouldn't it be so nice if God worked that way? If all of my wondering and fear and concern could be cooled and calmed in 90 days just because I decided it was so.

Although, if I were being honest to God, I would admit that I told him I was open to whatever. It could be that God had worked to inspire that boy to turn on that channel so he could offer me an invitation. What would it hurt if I took that lousy preacher as a sign—a wink and a smile from my facetious maker? Ha. He would. God is so cheeky. "Okay, God," I thought to myself, "Let's do it. 90 days. Let's see what you can do. You have 90 days to send me as many signs as you want. I'm listening."

Day 2 of 90: As the sun was rising, I was hiking. There was a small trail in town that perfectly accommodated a quick hike and exposed me to enough nature that I could reset. Walking at sunrise ensured I was also alone with my thoughts. It was just me and the sound of leaves rustling beneath my feet. So I thought. The trail was packed into a few small acres so the path made some abrupt switchbacks at different intervals. I rounded one such switchback and a doe, standing just feet in front of me, took my breath away. She stood frozen in the middle of the trail, her dark brown eyes were wide and locked with mine. Her coat was smooth and tan and her ear twitched atop her head. We both held our breath as we held our gaze until she leapt into the greenery beside her and immediately vanished.

Groping for my phone I typed in the search bar "Spiritual meaning of Deer."

Results:

Symbol of spiritual authority and connection between physical and spiritual realms.

Associated with the heart chakra, representing love, compassion and empathy

Invites reflection, grace, and trust in intuition

Oh shit. Is that a sign?

Day 9 of 90: I was driving home after class. It was dusk and I decided to cut through a different part of the neighborhood to prolong the commute and afford me more time to myself to process my day. My car lurched to a stop when I saw something moving in front of me. At first, I couldn't make it out, but then it turned to face me. An owl had fallen from the tree above and was getting his footing. He turned all the way around and looked directly at me while he spread his wings to their limits until both reached out wider than my car. With one little hop, he flew away. Hands shaking, I pulled the car to the side of the quiet street and got out my phone again.

"Spiritual Meaning of owls,"

Wisdom and inner knowing

Upcoming transitions or changes in your life

Explore inner wisdom

Okay then.

My phone rang in my hand and startled me. A friend was calling to tell me about this thing she had signed up for and she wanted me to come too. Her therapist was leading a Spiritual Retreat and she was too scared to go alone. With all the woodland creatures coming at me like I was Snow White, I figured I should. Two days after I signed up and paid for my spot, my friend backed out. Tricky signs. She was right, the thought of going alone was scary. But what could it hurt? Maybe it was just what I needed.

Day 22 of 90: The retreat was held in bed and breakfast not far from home. The front porch stretched from end to end across the face of the house. Kitschy decor from every era and religion was hung wildly along the walls and ceiling. Windcatchers danced in the breeze. Wooden chimes clapped out a cheery knocking. Colorful pillows covered every flat surface embroidered with pictures of the moon and stars. Buddhist flags stretched between the columns and little figurines of children and wildlife modeled themselves along the window sills in whimsical contortions. The foyer, decorated as thoroughly as the front porch, smelled of nag champa and essential oils. A woman with a messy bun and crooked glasses carried a clipboard as she scrambled to greet me. Checking my name on the list she directed me to the safari room.

The name did not disappoint. Wallpaper strewn with brown and green leaves covered the walls. A seven foot wooden sculpture of a giraffe kept watch from the corner. Ten or twelve pillows were piled at the head of the bed, each in a different animal print. The room definitely provided the same uneasy vulnerability I would imagine as sitting prey on a wildlife safari.

The space left me wondering if I had chosen poorly to come by myself. What awaited me in the coming days felt as unknown to me as a real life jungle, I was every bit an explorer in a strange land. I was smart enough to be afraid, but not yet experienced enough to know about what. My fellow explorers soothed some of my fears. Many of the others were therapists, each of us traveling alone, hunting our own trophy beasts.

Despite my room decor having nothing to do with the retreat itself, the theme of inner safari never left me. Through countless guided meditations, my inner guides would find themselves trudging through deep undergrowth feeling lost, looking for direction and meaning as they traveled. My heart truly was a dense jungle. At various points in the schedule we were asked to set an intention, or visualize a part of us that longed for healing and the vines of doubt and old beliefs would constrict around me, freezing me in indecision. The retreat was force-feeding me a painful reality: I was at a crossroads. Moving forward into an integrated and honest life was my deepest desire, but some truth, some fear was holding me back.

# 21

## Efflorescence

Bending the pages in between my fingers I read a list of words aloud to Brandi.

"Smart, funny, lighthearted, musical, has good hands and wears rings. Has interesting hobbies. That's an important one."

She had heard my complaints that I was not meeting quality men to date. So she recommended the age-old task of writing a list of the qualities I wanted. I reluctantly complied and made what I thought was a pretty unrealistic list. Before I could say "Abracadabra" the magic man materialized. Keith met nearly every trait. He loved music a lot and was a pretty talented musician himself. He thought I was an amazing singer (bonus). We agreed on the condition of modern Christianity, and we both loved a good drag show.

Day 29 of 90: Our first date was a casual lunch at a local cafe. He showed me his bright yellow mustang and spent the lunch working hard to impress me with his humor and successes. When it was my turn to speak, I did what every man loves and asked more about him. He was my height, stocky and bald. He had beautiful blue eyes and smiled with his whole mouth open.

Day 36 of 90: For our second date, he invited me to a bar. He was playing guitar in a band and I could drink for free all night. He was very talented and it did feel good to have him introduce me proudly to his band mates. I spent much of that evening alone at a table watching him play, seeing him look at me and make his best sexy face.

I knew how much Keith "*liked me*, liked me" and I felt some level of exhilaration watching him grow in his affinity for me. Could it be that my future husband had finally arrived? I willfully egged him on. I said all the right things. I was the perfect combination of flirty and vulnerable. It was totally working. It was the first time in a long time that I had found the power to attract what I wanted. He checked all the boxes, and I was free to fall in love.

I was not falling in love. There he was, everything I said I wanted and … nothing. Why couldn't I just let go and fall? What was this barrier in me? Perhaps it was some secret bisexual apprehension that my lack of heterosexual experience prevented me from understanding. My reluctance to fall in love with him could have been created by a fear that I would someday find a woman that felt irresistible. If I commit to this guy, I never get to touch a woman again. Would that be a problem? Who could I talk to about this?

Julie.

It had been a while since I was in her class. As semesters passed, she went from being my professor, to my clinical supervisor and the director of the clinic I was using to earn my practicum hours. I had grown to know her just enough to know that she would at least understand *what* I was asking even if she couldn't answer it. I had her number, so I texted.

*If a bisexual person chooses monogamy with one gender, will they spend the rest of their life missing the gender they didn't choose?*

Send.

Immediately I was filled with regret.

What the fuck, Jiggs? Why did I do that?

I shouldn't have asked that. That's too much. I've crossed some kind of line. She's my professor. I can't just send random shit. That's, like, probably too personal of me. That was dumb.

Fack.

Approximately 674 years later, she replied, "Let's talk about this in person."

Sleep evaded me that night. Between Keith texting me mushy messages and my deep self-loathing at being too needy with Julie I couldn't rest. Exhausted, I would have to go into the clinic the next morning for practicum, knowing that she would show up eventually and I would have to confront the fact that I asked such a weird question.

Day 37 of 90: She bustled into the office as she always did, and I tried hard to evaporate from the face of the planet. She disappeared into her office and I felt like perhaps I had become ephemeral. A few minutes later she popped her head out and motioned for me to join her. I felt sick. Nope. I was still here.

Our conversation was not long, it was not painful, and it was not complicated. It was a lot about knowing yourself, listening to yourself, and trusting yourself. I knew as she was saying it that these were not my strengths. I had grown up in doubt of myself. I was longing for rules and steps and procedures, and this was not that.

She was so kind to me even though I was a middle-aged woman asking middle-school questions about love and attraction. She saw my fear and embarrassment, but she didn't draw attention to it. Instead, she gently offered me a definition of these things that was completely devoid of convention or obligations. It was an expansive answer that left room for my input. It didn't require squeezing or eliminating or forcing. There were no rules telling me how to think, feel, hold my face, or how to stand or move.

"Listen Jiggs, I think you might be over-thinking things. It's not that complex. You just ask yourself simple questions and believe your answers. Do you like them? Do you want to spend a lot of time with them? Do you like the way they smell? Do you like the way they feel? Do you like the way they move? Do you want to be closer to them? Do you want to pull them closer to you?"

She rattled off the questions effortlessly. They all pointed in the same direction. Simple. Instinctual. Automatic. You weren't telling your body what to feel, you were asking it what it wanted. Everything was from the inside out, not the outside in. This was revolutionary.

"As for your question of longing for the gender you didn't pick, I don't know. I don't think it works like that. If you're attracted to both sexes, then you're really probably bonding more with a person's soul. It won't matter what body they are in. If you feel love and attraction, that can be more than enough to last forever. It sounds like you really just need to focus on whether or not you're attracted to the person you're currently dating."

Over the next several days, I considered all the moments of my life in light of that conversation. I had felt the desire alluded to in Julie's questions. I knew what it was to crave someone with my whole self. I still had vivid memories of the smells, sounds, and feelings I had experienced with the women I had loved. These weren't simply "pleasant elements" of enjoyable times. These were highly motivating forces that had genuine power over every logical, clear-headed thought I could think. It's not a matter of which fantasy I can muster up. It's a matter of which one I find impossible to turn off!

Day 41 of 90: I didn't tell Keith about that conversation. I didn't tell anyone about that conversation. He and I had tickets to a Joan Jett concert, and I really wanted to see her. He had it in his head that we could spend the night together after the concert and I didn't correct him. I felt compelled to do it. If I did, I could consider the answers to all of these new questions in real time. He showed up that night with very twinkly eyes and looked genuinely excited for the night ahead of us. We drove up a winding mountain road to the concert venue and laughed and talked. He told lots of stories about himself and asked about how things were going for me. Sigh. He was such a nice guy.

We held hands walking around the venue. I caught glimpses of us in mirrored columns and felt queasy seeing the reflection looking back at me. We didn't fit. Joan was amazing. She was nearing sixty and still a radiant badass. She danced around that stage kicking and screaming. Nothing could stop her. I was lost in her theatrics until this guy's sweaty little hand was groping around for mine. This goddess was giving us the performance of her life and you were still distracted by me? BAH! I was disgusted. I haunted myself with the thought that I would much rather go home with sixty-year-old Joan than sweaty McGee next to me, but I shook the thought from my mind. That was mean.

Once the concert ended, we headed for home, and I started to feel ill again. It was late and getting later. I knew exactly what was on his mind, and I was not excited. I mean, could I get excited? Should I invest some energy at working myself up so I would want to do it? Has it really been since high school that I was this close to doing this? Staring his offer in the face, I felt obligated to give it the old college try. I tried to focus. I tried to fantasize. I could do this. I could make it work. I could think about hot things and hot people and make myself want to touch him!

The drive coming down the mountain was much faster than the drive up it. Before I knew it, we were back at my place, and I had to choose one way or the other. Barricaded in the bathroom I sat on the edge of the tub thinking about Julie. She told me to listen to myself; to notice what I really wanted and believe what I felt. It was hard to know at that moment what I wanted. Many things floated to the surface. I wanted to know if I was attracted to men. I wanted to not hurt his feelings. I wanted to be normal. I wanted to be certain that I wasn't at all straight so that I didn't miss out on any sliver of opportunity to be normal. I wanted to sleep. I wanted to be by myself. I knew I didn't have to sleep with him to know I didn't care if I did or didn't.

Water danced over my fingertips as I waited for it to warm. I recalled my first kiss with Laci. That steamroller of a woman completely flattened my decision-maker. I not only didn't *have* to think, I couldn't. I thought about Mary. She led a parade of red flags that rivaled the opening ceremony at the Olympics and I couldn't resist her. I thought about Heather. All the morality and common sense, not to mention decades of friendship hanging in the balance, couldn't shake me from my desires. Was that the very point Julie was illustrating? Drying my hands in a towel, I looked at myself in the mirror. If there was even an ounce of me that was straight, I probably wouldn't have been able to resist every man's advances in twenty years of dating. Especially when I had never once resisted a woman for as much as 15 seconds.

Holy Shit.

"Oh no." I muttered coming out of my bathroom, Keith sitting nervously on the edge of my bed.

"What is it?" he asked as he rose to his feet.

"I just started getting a migraine. I get them when I drink certain alcohol. They start with little visual auras and within 15 minutes I have a blinding headache."

I wasn't lying, I did get migraines, and they did work like that. But I knew what triggered them and could take a couple painkillers and totally avoid the blinding headache part. I just needed a way out, and women have been blaming headaches for centuries. So, yeah, I was lying.

"Keith, I'm so sorry," I said, feeling teary, the apology was honest.

"What can I do? What do you need? Do you want to just go to sleep?"

Ugh. He was going to make me say it.

"I'm sorry, I think it's best if you just head home, I need to get to sleep before the headache starts and I don't know how I'll feel in the morning. I'm so sorry."

Now he was teary.

"Okay. If you're sure. I don't mind staying. I could bring you water."

"Not this time. Thank you. It's really sweet of you." Sigh, I was a bitch. I was a bitch and I'm going to hell for being bitchy to this nice man. Bless his heart.

My bed creaked as I sat down on it, he lingered to squeeze

my hand as he left and instructed me to get some sleep. I felt like shit. He turned back to flash his best puppy dog face and wave. Now I just *am* shit. No doubt. Every step he took away from me I felt more and more relieved that I didn't have to do what he wanted us to do. By the time his headlights flashed over my bedroom windows I felt the urgent need to talk to a friend.

I pulled out my phone and texted Charlotte. "Dude, I'm so fucking gay."

She texted back a laughing emoji and said, "Lol, I knew it!!"

There it was. The truth that had been planted in the ground during adolescence and slowly nurtured over the last year of self-acceptance had finally broken through the fresh healthy soil. Everything made sense. Had I really missed it all these years? What was I thinking? I wasn't a tomboy. I wasn't a late-bloomer. I wasn't super righteous. I wasn't even bi ... I was just a basic lesbian.

Day 42 of 90: I braced myself to make a very important call. I needed to tell Rosina. She liked the guy I was dating and was probably on pins and needles wanting to know how the date went. Hopefully she could handle the sudden change in direction.

"Jiiiiiiiggs," She answered on the first ring, "tell me eeeevrythiiiiiing."

"Okay," I laughed. "But just brace yourself, it's not what you're expecting."

"Okay, okay, I'm braced, spill it!"

"We didn't do it. I sent him home. I faked a headache."

"What?! Jiggs! What happened?!"

"Rose..." long pause...cleansing breath, "I think I'm just gay dude. I just couldn't"

I barely had the confession out of my mouth before she was busy demonstrating her love with compassionate words and reassurances.

"Jiggs, you're my bestie and I love you. If you want to be gay...no wait... if you think you're gay...no wait... If you're gay that's awesome. Jeez louise, sorry for the awkward, I'm growing over here."

I laughed at her, "Thanks Rose. I love you too."

"Can I say one thing and you won't be mad?"

"Sure."

"I dunno, Jiggs, maybe you just shouldn't write this guy off too hastily. Aren't you just a little curious about what it's like? I feel like if you just did it one time you could know for sure that it wasn't for you."

I snickered hearing her say out loud what I had just believed the night before.

"I hear ya, but can I ask *you* one question?"

"Sure! Sure!"

"Do you need to sleep with just one girl to know you don't want to?"

She roared with laughter. "Touche, Jiggs! Touche! And now I feel silly for asking such a silly question! Thank you my Jiggs! You are gay and it's okay!" She sang her words as though they were a peppy jingle.

Day 49 of 90: I knew with unshakeable certainty that she needed to know everything. My heart trusted hers to understand and have compassion, but I couldn't still my trembling hands as I stood before her a few days later about to share in stark honesty what had happened with Mary and Heather. I had lied to her all those years ago. In the midst of Mary, I had even attempted to gaslight her vivid memories.

These wouldn't be just names in a story to her, they were real people. Some of them were even still her friends. There was a reasonable chance that she would be hurt by these revelations. I could very well have done irrevocable damage to her trust. I had lost important people to these stories before.

Any worry I had about her questioning our entire relationship was washed away at her immediate and decisive response. She defended me, angry at others, and that deep compassion that has always been an essential component to her character was even bigger and bolder. She said the distance she had felt between us at various points all those years made sense now and she was so sorry I went through all of it alone. I worried aloud that her reaction was too biased, and encouraged her to consider being mad at me or judging me a little bit. I deserved that. She brushed off my invitation and said she was grateful that she had grown enough to still get to stand beside me as I found myself. She was honored that I trusted her enough to share the shameful parts. And she was excited to talk shit about anyone who hurt me.

It's a wonder that this woman was my friend. Life is such a winding road of ups and downs. Rosina proved time and time again to be a compass that always pointed me toward the true north. Because of her, I could never doubt that God existed, or that God was loving. Only a compassionate and omnipotent force could have designed someone so perfectly suited to be my friend. It was a miracle that God would then set Rosina on a path all her own that somehow always synchronized with mine. No matter how she conceptualized what made a person good, there was always enough room for me. Regardless of how little contact we had or how different our experiences, her growth kept a steady pace with mine, so that neither of us could wander far, and neither of us were alone. She is my soul's companion. If everyone from that moment on rejected me, I would be okay.

It was this series of events, in the space held open for me by loving teachers and therapists, as my hand fanned away the settling dust of my deconstructed faith, my real self, like a stubborn dandelion from a crack in the concrete, had opened itself to me. I knew without doubt, without fear, without shame, exactly who I was. I saw who God, in all her wisdom, had created me to be, and I was as beautiful and perfect as any other flower in the garden.

# 22

# Revelation

Day 80 of 90: In the midst of all of this revelation and exposure I was invited to another spiritual retreat like the one I had gone on a month earlier. Knowing the size and scope of my own recent awakenings, I felt sure that this retreat would be so much more powerful. A vision for my life was appearing, and the nature of the work ahead of me was clear. I had plenty of intentions to set, and plenty of vision to cast for myself.

We met this time at a cabin deep in the Pisgah forest. The space was clean and open. Very few decorations hung on the walls, the owner choosing instead to let the giant picture windows create the mood. Light filled the rooms and no distinct fragrances hung in the air. The people with me were women of various ages, all equipped with wild eyes and grounded hearts.

The weekend was packed with interesting activities meant to provoke emotion and generate rich symbolism to free us from unhelpful or destructive narratives. Some of these rituals involved creating what hadn't previously existed, and some served to cleanse or clear what didn't belong. Two times that weekend, the moment called on the power of fire.

The leader invited us to search our inner world and locate something that no longer served us. Was there a story, a belief, or a habit that we just knew in our bones was creating more harm than good? She supplied implements to create little bundles as we meditated. We were instructed to make a bundle from little crumpled nests of paper, and add any natural elements we wished to symbolize this thing, this problem we intended to eliminate. We were to toss the bundles into the fire and watch them vanish in the flames and invited to visualize the same thing occurring to the burden it symbolized inside of us.

We were given time to sit and reflect. I stared at the mountain in the distance and thought back on the whirlwind of events that had swept me up over the last few months. There were so many huge differences in how I was defining myself, but I felt more like me than I ever had. My identity was crystalizing, and all that was left was completely embodying her. There were still places in my life where I wasn't honest with myself. My family didn't know I was gay. My job would fire me if they knew. Being gay wasn't a new thing, it was just a thing I spent all those years hiding, even from myself! That's what I needed to burn. Hiding. It was a necessary strategy for a long time, but it had grown problematic. All this time I blamed God for my life not going well. He had been punishing me for being gay or being weak. But really, my life hadn't materialized because I hadn't been living it. I had been hiding.

In a folded brown paper bundle, I sprinkled sage leaves, rose petals, and little granules of frankincense. Closing it up with my thumbs I closed my eyes and whispered a little prayer to myself.

"Tonight, in honor of my future and all it can be, I'm letting go of hiding."

Sparks raced toward the sky as I tossed in my bundle. It toppled down the burning wood and nestled into the pile of ash at the bottom of the fire. I watched the paper turn black as flames licked and devoured the contents. A gentle curl of smoke swirled upward and into the sky. Tears turned colder as they fell down my cheeks thinking about how difficult it was going to be to not hide. Exposure is scary.

Day 84 of 90: The leader instructed us to walk the grounds of the retreat center and find something in nature to represent our intentions for the new year. Fire that night would be used, not as a destructive force, but as a transistor. It would transform our offerings into a smoke that would rise to the new moon and mix with the power of nature to manifest the intentions they symbolized. My heart laughed at the hippy witchiness of it all. How mortified my former self would have been.

Plodding along the frozen ground crunching on twigs and ice, it captured me. In the cold earth, after long periods of rain and snow all weekend, there it was, flowering close to the ground: one little dandelion. It grew there in the frozen mud surrounded by last summer's dying grass, still too tenacious to quit. It was determined to bloom and flower regardless of the harsh environment it endured. It was entirely out of season, out of character, out of rebellion.

God, I wanted to be that damn flower. I wanted to be myself to my fullest potential, open to the sky, grounded in the earth, and determined to grow despite lacking support or ideal conditions. There is a great deal of irony in my hastily plucking that one little flower out of the ground and killing it in a fire, but that day that flower grew there especially for me. That flower and I had the same intentions. Later that night, with the stars and nine feral ladies as my witness, I tossed my intentions into the fire and declared that I would grow, where I was, into what I was, regardless of the harshness of the conditions around me. I declared myself a dandelion and celebrated.

# 23

# Okay, Cupid

Day 89 of 90: Signs had come in abundance. Everything felt truly magical. I know, I absolutely could have been making it up, but I wasn't making up the peace I felt as everything had unfolded. I sat on the edge of my bed, clutching my phone, staring at a dating app. After a deep breath, I carefully selected Women seeking Women. I wasn't totally sure how to live the life I was walking into, but I was excited to learn. I had been in relationships with women and felt pretty competent in that area, but I had never publicly dated one. I had also never had a relationship with a professional lesbian. I had avoided real friendship with lesbians most of my life, because, you know, homophobia. All of the women I had been in love with were either "confused" or married to men. I was, at best, a part-time, amateur lesbian.

What decent, grown, lesbian woman would be patient and kindly escort me across all those thresholds I had yet to cross? For the trace amounts of doubt left about my sexual identity, I still had immense doubt about moving forward to live it out. I convinced myself that I was jumping into shark-infested waters. It took a while to realize that shark-infested waters are not scary if you too are a shark.

My time in the water taught me that women weren't any better than men when it came to sending inappropriate pics, half-assed offers, and "w y d?" instead of real conversation. I talked to a lot of women and eventually started having flashbacks of every man I had ever dated. I had assumed dating women would be easier. My head was filled with visions of women running after me with insatiable lust in their eyes while I fended them off with a big stick. Surprisingly, this did not happen. Additionally, the lesbian community is, how should we say, tight-knit. Once a woman knew what town I called home, the questions would begin:

"Oh, do you know Vicky and them?" she inquired.

"Um nope, I don't think so," I replied.

"Oh, how bout Rhonda and Tess? They're pretty popular." suspicions of me grew.

"No, huh-uh."

Every woman did it. They needed to link me to someone. Lesbians in the south were a rare commodity, so if you had been in more than one relationship, you could connect yourself to another lesbian with very few degrees of separation. Who you had dated was also used as a predictor of the future success of your budding relationship. If you hit it off with Jackie, you would probably hate Maggie. But it might mean you would be a great fit with Jan. Ugh. Poor Jan though, it's a shame about her and Betty. Everybody knew everything about everybody else. It seemed I was the proud owner of the biggest possible red-flag a lesbian could have: anonymity.

I managed to go out with a few women, but only went out a second and third time with one. Her name was Anna and she was pretty weird. I know I was becoming a therapist, but that doesn't mean that I can't judge certain behaviors as way too out of bounds for me. She was attractive. She had a small frame and blonde hair. She had big doe-y blue eyes that she held in a constant pout. I had no trouble watching her move and enjoying the view. But I did find myself fighting back a daze of boredom when she talked about her life's many dramatic entanglements.

Not only was I now dating the opposite sex from before, but I was experiencing the opposite problems. I had managed to find a few men with good jobs from good families who were very nice and paid attention to me, but I never felt attracted to them. I usually got out of those relationships quickly because it didn't seem fair. It was easy to end things devoid of chemistry regardless of how perfect the man seemed. But stick me with a woman who stored weed in her bra, that she had to smoke to reduce her anxiety about the state of her life as she was not able to afford her bills unless she did unsavory favors for the guy living in her basement and somehow I find it hard to make a choice because, well, she's kinda cute. I guess this is why my straight friends would always seem to fall for the wrong guys. Surprisingly, she would end up rejecting me. While this did hurt briefly, my future self carries the memory with much relief for what might have been, but never was. To relieve the hurt, my friends and I dubbed her "spanks her nanny." No special reason.

One afternoon, when heading back from a kayaking day with Kristen, my phone alerted me. I was driving and didn't recognize the tone, so I had her check it for me. She said it was a dating app notification. Someone had messaged me. She started bouncing in the seat chanting, "Let me look! Let me look!" She knew my passcode and I gave her permission. She read the profile outloud and I kept my eyes on the road.

"Liza. 36. An RN. She has a wiener dog! Yeah! She loves dogs, that's awesome! Taylor could have a brother!" Kristen already liked her.

"Okay, Okay, keep reading."

"Okay. She says she likes mountain biking and spending time with friends. She loves family and music. Just kinda generic stuff. She didn't answer all the questions. But she's so cute, look how cute!" She shoved the phone in front of my face so I could glance. From the quick glimpse I saw a cute happy face on the body of a regular, healthy person. She didn't have blue hair, or face piercings, and she wasn't ripped and tan, or a wilting waif of a woman.

"Yeah, she's cute! So did she message me? What's it say?'

"Oh yeah, okay. She says "Hey Jennifer, thought your profile was interesting. Cool that you play music, what kind of music do you play?" Ooooo lemme write her back!! Please Please!"

"Sure...umm. I guess just say, "Hi Liza, I liked your profile too. I mostly play acoustic girl music. What kind of music do you like?""

The rest of our ride home Kristen played the part of my personal secretary typing out a conversation that I would eventually take over and continue well into the night and into the next day. Liza was so easy to talk to and asked thoughtful questions that kept conversation feeling alive and interesting. Every time the notification light would blink I would smile expectantly hoping it was from her. Only a couple of days into texting she asked if we could talk on the phone.

I winced. I hate talking on the phone. It's so tough for me. There's no time to think about the best reply and there are so many things that can happen around me and distract me from the conversation. I did not want to call. But I did want to hear how her voice sounded. It was just a matter of time before I would have to anyway. Might as well get the first time over with. I agreed and she called almost immediately.

"Helloooo?" I said that so weird.

"Hey this is Liza!" Ohmygod, her name was Leeeza. Not Lie-za. Yikes. I hope I don't fuck that up. She had such a nice voice though. It was deep and confident. I was ready to just keep talking to this Miss Leeeza.

Contrary to my phone anxiety we spent two hours talking that night. The conversation was good, but her laugh was what kept me talking. She had the best laugh. It was sweet and silly and bubbled right from her heart. I would tell a joke and she would chuckle and tell one right back, and I would chuckle and take the joke a bit further and we both would cackle. The back and forth would continue until one of us pushed the comedy slightly over the line and we would both grow quiet in the awkwardness. One of us would comment, "too far," and we would burst into laughter all over again.

Talking to her was nice. She was so honest and outspoken, it was a big change from how I approached life. It felt inspiring to see things from her perspective. It wasn't long before we set up a first date. She texted me and explained that she didn't want to build too much of a relationship on our phones just in case we didn't have any chemistry in person. She thought it was a good idea to at least meet up and make sure we really liked each other. So pragmatic. Not yet confident in my own snap decision making, I flashed a picture of her to a therapist friend walking by and blurted out, "Hey, she just asked me out, should I say yes?"

"Hmm," he paused, looking at the image, "Um, absolutely, Yes."

# 24

# Liza

April 25th, the day I met Liza. The trees along the drive were proudly displaying their fresh young leaves and the evening sun twinkled yellows and oranges on the cars ahead of me. The weather perfectly captured the tone of my heart with its fresh spring hopefulness. We were meeting in the middle for dinner. During my drive I fought back worries about everything from my appearance to which stories I should tell to seem interesting. Attempting to occupy myself with math, I calculated and recalculated the time and distance before I would arrive. I chewed the inside of my cheek as I pulled into a parking spot.

As I walked toward the restaurant I saw her. Fifteen long steps of awkward smiles and we met with a hello and quick hug. I was relieved. She was every bit as cute in real life as she had been in her pictures. She walked with an understated but confident swagger. She wore a nice sweater with a hint of glitter in the fabric, and dark fitted jeans. Her outfit fit nicely around her curves. Her eyes were dark and piercing. They were sizing me up and approving.

She invited me into conversations about hobbies, and family. We took turns sharing, neither wanting to hog the attention. Her stories were rich and colorful. With every passing moment I felt my shoulders relax and my spine unlock. Before long our plates were pushed away, elbows on the table and our laughter loud and hearty. It wasn't the kind of comfort I felt with friends, although it was akin to it. This was a deep desire to be my complete self with her. I wanted to pull my hair back, wear a T-shirt, and talk shit. Her stability and energy made me want to be more of myself than any other date I had ever been on. Her curiosity encouraged my disclosure. Her anecdotes intrigued me. Her giddy chuckle richly rewarded my every joke. This level of connection was scary, but I was choosing to "fuck it" and flat out say what was on my mind the way my therapist had challenged me. Contrary to the anticipated outcome of all of my fears being realized as she ran away in the distance, it seemed the more I pressed into authenticity, the more interested she got, the more she leaned toward me. It felt the same for me too.

Touches were rare during dinner. Just an occasional hand on the arm or a close lean when showing each other pictures. The desire was there, but fear was also. It was a fear that other people would see and express disgust. It would be a shame if self-righteous strangers ruined such a beautiful night. Better to let the self-consciousness of potential judgment ruin the evening than becoming a bonafide victim of a hate crime.

The waitress asked how we wanted the check and I knew the date was coming to an end, something I wasn't ready to do. Thinking I had figured out an adorable way to keep it going, I made an observation.

"You know it stinks that we live so far apart.".

"Yeah, but this drive wasn't too bad. It was worth the trip."

"Yes, totally. The tough part though, is that by the time we can schedule this again, it may have been a while and even though it would only be our actual second date, it might feel more like our third or fourth date."

"Sure, that's probably true," she was trying to work out where the hell I was headed.

"So, what I think we should do is maximize the time we can see each other. Like tonight, let's call this restaurant date one, and then we can change locations and call it date two. That is, if you'd want to go on a second date with me."

She laughed, "Okay, so you want to go on a second date right now?"

"Yes! And I know just the place!"

She was kind to humor me. Thinking I knew this city well, I remembered a park nearby that was just beautiful. We could go there and look at the stars or walk under the street lamps. It would be so romantic! A confusing maze of one-way streets and a u-turn or two later and Liza started squirming.

"You're not taking me to a back alley to kill me are you?" Ohmygod I was ruining it! "No no. Haha. I just can't find the place I was thinking about."

One more loop around the scary industrial buildings and I gave up.

"I can't find it," I sighed, "It was a cute little park. It was going to be awesome."

Scanning my map for a new place to go, I was embarrassed and anxious and being weird. Restaurant after Restaurant showed closed, or closing soon. There was a noisy bar full of college students, or the same place we had just been.

"I don't suppose I could interest you in another date at the same place we just left."

She laughed, "We could sit outside and have a few more."

A credit to her laid-back style, our second date was at a picnic table outside at the same restaurant drinking beers. A live band was playing that consisted of two middle aged people, a woman on keyboards and a man on guitar. They were good enough to listen to when conversation lulled, but not so good that they distracted us from each other. By the second beer on our second date we both had our hair pulled back and were laughing like old friends.

She walked me to my car and I chattered relentlessly awkward nothingness the entire way there. She stood patiently by the side of the car swaying back and forth from her heels to her toes waiting for me to shut up. At some point she realized I may never and she interrupted me. She raised a finger in the air like a student trying to get the teacher's attention and said, "I'm sorry, can I just…"

Then she pulled me toward her by the waist and kissed me. I was relieved and thrilled to find that waiting for us in that kiss was all the spark we could ever need. Everything else that night had gone so well, and I was so afraid that something would be lingering somewhere that might foil this perfect night, and now we were here, kissing in the dark parking lot. She was smart, rational, employed, funny and hot. I was 35 and it was the first time I was on a date with one person who had everything I wanted.

"I think that was a good first date!" She had called on the trip home.

"Technically a good first and second date."

"Haha, yeah first and second date. I hope I can see you again?"

"Yes, we definitely will," I replied.

We met the next week in another city between us. The week after that I drove to her house. The week after that she came to meet me in my city. Before I knew it, she was my first real girlfriend. She seemed so perfect for me. I wondered if perhaps I was blinded to her flaws, or if I had dated such bad women before that normal people flaws had become camouflaged to me. Her confidence intimidated me, but I loved it. She was successful, especially compared to me, but also compared to most other 30 somethings. She knew exactly whose opinions mattered and she was not afraid to ask those people for advice. If I expressed concern about the opinions of people she didn't think mattered she offered no hesitation in reminding me that those people could fuck off. In fact, she made it seem like the most logical response in the world. Why hadn't I ever thought to do that?

The only thing that struck me as odd about my relationship with Liza was the calm, natural way it unfolded. For all of the years I had spent in focused and intense self-doubt, I felt zero hesitation when it came to spending time with her. Dating men always included a near constant level of second guessing, polling every decision and action with a crowd of at least five straight women to discern whether or not I was behaving appropriately. It wasn't attraction. It was method acting. Of course, my relationships with other women were tangled rat's nests of deception; precarious tight-rope acts of seeming appropriate, careful not to let too much truth escape my lips and spoil the next secret meeting. None of that happened with Liza. She just made me happy. She only wanted me to know her friends and family. She wanted to spend every moment with me. She wanted to hold my hand. The effortlessness of real love was shocking.

# 25

# Commencement

Graduation is a very public celebration of a very personal accomplishment. Each student crosses the stage inspired by their own motivations, having conquered their own unique struggles. None of us understands the race of the person next to us, but we all arrive at the same moment to cross the finish line together. Pulling onto campus for the last time, regalia swinging in the back window, a myriad of feelings swirled in my chest. It was exciting to think that I had completed something that for nearly two decades I had decided was impossible. I felt such pride at having fought hard for something that could never be taken away from me. But the struggle and the pace had become a lifestyle. My classmates had become my community. This ceremony was the final bar in a song that had inspired me to dance and I was sad it was coming to an end.

The click of my steps on the sidewalk toward the auditorium pulsed with more confidence than those I made on the way to my admission interview. I was not the same woman. Every professor, every class, every lecture inspired me to ask more of myself: more courage, more compassion, more curiosity. It taught me well the skills of viewing others with unconditional positive regard, yes. But more importantly it birthed an entirely new part of me capable of giving myself the same unique kind of affection. I learned how to care for myself, how to protect myself from other people's sharp edges. I felt free to experiment with ideas, and lean into new experiences. Risks were allowed and I was strong enough to deal with their consequences.

In the decades prior, the Church had systematically robbed me of an inner voice I could trust. My former self was anxious, afraid of messing up and afraid of letting people down. She believed she was fundamentally broken and her shitty life was proof that she dwelt at the receiving end of God's judgmental wrath. She was vulnerable to the ideologies of others because she found it hard to trust her gut. She sought something she didn't actually want: a relationship with a man, in order to obtain what she needed: belonging. What school and therapy had taught me was that by squeezing myself into what didn't actually fit, I was pushing that sense of belonging farther away.

Honesty is a frightening and costly strategy. It makes you vulnerable to rejection, judgment and attack. It can expose your ignorance and folly and put you at risk for manipulation. It can hurt people, disappoint and anger them. Despite the popular discourse, our collective private reality remains: there are many good and honorable reasons to lie and most of us do it with staggering frequency. We change the frame around it, calling it polite, considerate, or private. But we crave a wide and sturdy mask behind which we can store our weaker, needier selves. We have grown deeply devoted to the grand performance, manufacturing and peddling a version of ourselves that might heal our unique brand of suffering.

When my performance as a straight christian failed me, I blamed my broken inner lesbian for sabotaging us. She was at fault. She was the problem. Living in a community of therapists encouraged me to sit with her instead. I learned to care about her, and care for her. My acceptance of her made becoming her less frightening, and the possible rejection from others less catastrophic. Owning her, being her, also made acceptance from others sweeter. I never second-guessed someone's affection for me when they knew about her. There was no secret lingering in the dark that had the power to turn the tables on me. I was free to be myself, open to genuine acceptance and fully capable of managing the pain of any rejection one might force upon me.

Meeting Liza was as much of a commencement as receiving my degree. The version of me who started grad school would have been too self-conscious and simultaneously self-unconscious to have even been Liza's friend. My love for her was so deeply symbolic of the hard work I had done to examine myself, deconstruct poisonous parts of my faith and accept and love myself. RuPaul was right, if you can't love yourself, how the hell are you gonna love somebody else?

Grief and joy danced around me as my friends pressed their cheeks to mine for selfies after the ceremony. Fear visited briefly when professors would sing my praises to my parents, reminding me that there were still secrets unrevealed. Nostalgia showed up early, like an excited new tenant measuring for their furniture. She would be moving in soon and this would all be a memory. I took mental pictures. Remember that building. Don't forget that face. Enjoy this moment, deeply enjoy it. The path that stretched beyond graduation unfolded before me, exciting and overwhelming, and I was prepared.

# 26

# Pride

"Pride comes before destruction, a haughty spirit before the fall." Proverbs 16:18. "God opposes the proud but gives grace to the humble." James 4:6. Christians were clear about pride. Bad, bad, bad. It was a double sin that the LGBTQ community called it Gay Pride. Not only was Pride month a disgusting display of debaucherous hedonism, but it was sinful to rejoice in yourself. Only bad things happen there and no good Christian should ever be a part of it. When Liza invited me to her town for pride weekend, an old part of me expected the worst.

Her friends annually threw a bash they lovingly called the "Big Gay Pool Party." Just ten or twelve people lounging around a pool, grilling and being fabulous. Her friends had heard all about me and were very excited to meet me in real life. So, on a hot sunny day in June, I found myself poolside smiling nervously, fielding personal questions from strangers as I bobbed in the water. Pools weren't my favorite place as swimsuits displayed more of my body than I cared to expose, but I was surprised by how comfortable things felt. Apparently gay men don't make me nearly as self-conscious as straight ones. By the afternoon, I was just sitting around a pool noshing on a chicken leg with all my chub showing. It was fantastic!

Liza's friends were delightful. They were silly and warm and told embarrassing stories about her and themselves. They recalled horrible hikes and disastrous love affairs. At various moments, each one would catch me by myself and tell me about how wonderful their friend was and how much they could tell she liked me. It was the same comfort that I experienced when I first met Liza, these people felt like home, like family.

Arriving back at her house after the party, my heart was full of warm goodness, and my back was covered in warm sunburn. Liza explained that the next morning we would need to get up and have breakfast before attending the parade. I was filled with excitement! I *love* a parade! The marching bands and the smiling people atop beautiful floats waving and tossing candy; parades always made me cry. My anxiety held my sleep back just long enough to scare me with visions of this parade being like a sado-masochistic circus of horrors, at the end of which Satan would drag us all to hell. It seemed I might have more work to do with Brandi.

As the hot summer sun heated the streets of downtown, I stood amongst the crowd, clutching my pride flag and wiping tears from my cheeks. Drum beats rang through the air that smelled of car exhaust and popcorn. Floats crawled past filled with people of every shape and color. Children squealed as they ran from the sidewalk gathering candy that had bounced on the ground nearby. Everyone waved and smiled. At first glance, this parade was just like every other: happy people happily celebrating a happy occasion. But it wasn't the same.

A closer inspection revealed a deeper truth about what was

happening around us. An older man walked the parade route wearing a shirt that said "Free Dad Hugs" and young people ran to him for an embrace, some weeping for their own estranged fathers. Butch women rolled by on thick growling motorcycles tossing tootsie rolls. Thin men in pastel polos and khaki shorts held hands while toddlers slept in carriers strapped to their chests. A flatbed truck rolled by filled with hippies beating out a slow rhythm on buffalo drums. This was a parade filled with all the people not invited to all the other parades. There was little space for these folks in traditional society. They belonged here. They were celebrated. They marched to prove their existence. Every person walking by me that day was a different story of the same struggle to love themselves and find joy in being different from the world. We came together that day to witness each other and declare our solidarity, we were not broken, and we were not alone. It was such an honor to be with them. It was an honor to be one of them.

High on pride, I pushed our relationship forward. Rosina had been continually begging me to meet Liza. It was definitely time to let them meet one another and I felt confident that she would earn Rosina's seal of approval. We scheduled dinner at a Mexican restaurant near Rosina's house. I introduced them and watched Rosina work her magic. I'm introverted and awkward most of the time but Rosina has always been the yin to my yang. She can talk a hole through a rug, and she can dig to the core of a person in a brief dialogue. As I watched these two worlds of mine collide, I saw in Rosina's expression a growing relief. She had confessed to me beforehand that she was nervous to meet Liza because, from what she had seen, I had horrible taste in women. She knew she could only be honest with me and was convinced that she would have to tell me that Liza was crazy. She was able to let that guard down soon after the introductions when she discovered Liza was a sane, balanced, and happy person. Once she discovered that Liza was a catch, she turned her concern to me, advising me not to wreck it.

As the leaves started to drop from the branches Liza attempted to lighten our nightly phone conversation with a joke.

"So are you going to bring me home to meet your parents for Thanksgiving?" she asked.

For the first time in our relationship, reluctance chilled its way up my spine and I felt the old familiar gnawing of fear in my belly.

"What? That's in just a couple months!"

"Well, you've met mine! Don't tell me you're ashamed of me!" She was very obviously joking but I was too afraid to laugh.

She had introduced me to her family less than a month after meeting. She had no problem exposing them to me and me to them. There was no hesitation or fear. She held no secrets or mysteries from her family. I still did. My parents were so kind and loving, these two sides of my world would have a great time together as long as my parents didn't mind that she was a woman. But it was such a big deal. Could I really come out to them, tell them I was dating someone, and ask them to host her within six weeks? That's a lot of adjustment in a short period of time. I mean, it took me 35 years to accept the truth. They might need some time too.

"I can't do it. I'm sorry. It's a lot for me and it gives me a lot of anxiety. I have to do this at my own pace and I will not be pushed!" I snapped.

"Umm…okay," her words part scolding, part defensive, "First of all, I was kidding and second, I already have plans so don't worry. I'm not trying to force you to introduce me. Whatever."

I wilted.

"I'm sorry. I'm so sensitive about this subject. And honestly I have been thinking about this subject for a while. I've just never been in this situation before. I've never dated anyone I liked enough to bring home. I don't know how to do it. But I know I need to soon."

I was fawning. Whatever she was feeling, I didn't like. I wanted us to repair whatever damage I had done. I pressed to know what she was thinking. She waved off the investigation insisting that she was fine and it wasn't a big deal.

Whether she felt it was a big deal or not, I did. I knew a revelation was calling.

A few weeks later on what seemed an average Tuesday I was having lunch outside with a good friend. I was open with my fears, and she commiserated. She remembered revealing similar things to her parents. It's hard to be honest when we are afraid of the worst case scenario. She also told me that it was probably synchronistic that I was talking to her about it that day. It was October 11th: National Coming Out Day. She said it would be poetic and an act of solidarity with the thousands of other queers confronting the same fear.

I thought about all of the people from the pride parade, those marching, those watching, those receiving free mom and dad hugs. For some of them, this moment was truly harrowing. Some of them were kicked out of their homes, abandoned by people who were supposed to love them unconditionally. Some were forced to attend abusive conversion therapies, or physically beaten by homophobic parents. In some parts of the world coming out means jail time, or a death sentence. I didn't know that my parents would accept me completely, or let Liza come for a holiday, but I at least had the comfort of being a fully self-sustaining adult in a country that wasn't actively persecuting me. If Mom and Dad rejected me, it would hurt, but I wouldn't die.

I'll be honest here. I wanted it to be over, but I sure didn't want to do it. I wanted to bring Liza home and have it be as normal as bringing home a friend. It had been agonizing for me to make the journey from one paradigm to another and I honestly didn't want my sweet parents to have to go through that themselves. My heart knew they should hear it from me at home in person where I was available to answer any questions. The facial expressions, sighs and awkward pauses were all mine to take on the chin. But I also wanted for them to have a minute with space for their own genuine reaction and free from the pressures of protecting my feelings. Who knows now if it was a good choice but I sent them a text telling them I was dating a girl and they could feel however they wanted or needed to, but I was going to do this. It was "fuck-it" lite. Same taste, fewer calories.

Texting is the worst. The whole world stops turning as you play every possible worst case scenario through your head while staring at the message you sent. You play a round of candy crush, watch a couple videos, even try putting your phone away and distracting yourself with reality. The tension holds until you finally receive the reply you crave. I don't remember now how long it was exactly. Eternity passed, that's for certain.

The first message back was mixed. I was always loved, but it was disappointing. That's cool, you know? I expected that much. I really did. I was deeply familiar with where my parents were coming from, and I knew that this was not going to be an instantly supportive situation. Also, I was rapidly approaching forty by this point and there wasn't much they could do to change it. The follow up messages over the next few days increased in their love and acceptance. By Christmas they had invited her to dinner.

The familiar crunch of gravel welcomed us as we turned into my parent's house. The car bumped and shook over the dirt driveway that always washed away in patches despite my Dad's best efforts to level it. Their little white house on the hill was at least 100 years old. The original floor plan was four rooms: two bedrooms, a living room and a kitchen. When the time came, the owners added indoor plumbing. Later my Dad built a den. It was modest, but after all the work we had put into it, 100% us. Mom had added her usual candles in the window for the holidays. A bushy green wreath greeted us at the door. The backdoor opened with the jingle of sleigh bells Mom had hung on the knob.

Mom was sitting in her rocker, longing to scratch the paint from her nails, but resisting. She rose to greet me and my guest. After a hug, Liza handed her a bag of candies and a compliment on her decorations. The kitchen was three steps higher than the den making my Dad twelve inches more intimidating as he dried his hands on his apron in the doorway. He brought himself down to our level and offered everyone a hug and asked about our trip. Mom offered us a drink and I offered myself a cleansing breath. The scariest part was over. My brother and sister were waiting in the living room and welcomed Liza with cheers and hugs.

Everyone remained on their best behavior the entire day. It was surreal watching my family interact with someone I was dating. It hadn't happened since high school, and maybe everyone thought it never would. It felt right. I felt like a grown up. Mom led Liza on a guided tour of the Christmas tree ornaments, being careful to highlight my cutest creations. Dad took her on a walk through the fields and showed her my favorite tree while I watched from the window emotionally eating Christmas cookies. Brother and Sister showed her family albums and spilled all of the family secrets, only the strangest and most hilarious, of course. Mom and Dad even made sure there were presents under the tree for her despite not knowing much about her. Liza reported that it was a lovely day, and Mom and Dad affirmed that she was a lovely girl. The tears that fell on my cheeks as we drove back to Liza's were evidence that we had achieved a perfect case scenario.

Once my parents met her, there was nothing to stop me from posting about us on social media. My heart saw this as the last and final step in really coming out. These spaces were diverse conglomerations of friends and acquaintances I had gathered over the last several decades. Childhood friends, coworkers from old jobs, professors, pastors, friends' parents, cousins, all gathered there. To be out in this space meant that my identity would be public record. It meant that people who meant little to me would get to judge me privately and at no cost to them. Worst case, people could attack me with their opinions. I pressed onward. Not a minute after tagging Liza as my partner, like after like started pouring in. I know we aren't supposed to be consumed with how many "likes" we get, but on that day, I stayed fixated on just that. Each "like" burned into my brain, an inventory of who truly supported me. A few people normally active on my page were suspiciously silent. My friend count went down by three, though I still haven't figured out which three.

Surprisingly, some of the hardest people to stop worrying about were the missionaries still in residence in Croatia. The story I had written was that they had watched me since I left, invested in me turning out okay. The avatars I had created of them waited for me to finally marry a guy and have kids already. Laci had already done that. She did it within a couple years of returning home. Broadcasting my sexual identity on social media meant they saw it and then they would know that the debacle was my fault. The jury would conclude that Jennifer was the gay problem that innocent Laci couldn't untangle. Their likes didn't show up among the rest.

Behind the scenes that year, another very interesting thing happened. Somewhere in Croatia, a young man previously unknown to me, uploaded that old worship CD and made it available online. It's currently at 3 million views and counting. When I found out about its popularity, I'll admit, I thought of Laci. All of her passionate determination had worked. Millions of people had heard me. I was as close to a rockstar as I would ever get.

Friends still in Croatia would reach out and share in my excitement. Locals practically begged me to come back and do a concert. They could get so many people to attend! It was some time after posting about my relationship that I decided to be bold and offer the missionaries that I come and do just that, reminding them that Liza would be with me. They declined, citing the rules of the ministry restricting them from associating with me formally because of my "lifestyle."

My better qualities might always prevent me from being completely free of concern about other people's judgment. Every thought I think and decision I make is up for interpretation and we are all free to decide if we think someone is right or wrong, good or bad. Are we living at all if there aren't some people who disagree with us? Accepting that truth would surely benefit me. My head knows that. But it doesn't prevent it from breaking my heart from time to time when people declare me unfit.

Pride is a powerful force. The courage shared with me by countless others at that parade had done its work in me. I saw that there was a tribe willing to love me if everyone I loved rejected me and that empowered me to take the leap toward myself. Regardless of who approved or who didn't, I had done it. No more closet doors. After 25 years of hiding myself, distorting myself and denying my identity, I was finally out. I was just gay. Curiously, the world kept spinning. There was no mushroom cloud, the sky did not fall. Some people left, but most stayed. Everyone just went on about their lives and I got to move forward into my own.

# 27

# Golden Hour

In the early morning of March 23rd, just shy of three years from our first date, I carefully slid out of bed and put on the clothes I had draped over a chair the night before. The fancy hotel key slipped into my back pocket and I snuck out of the room, careful to not let the heavy door slam and wake anyone. I drove to the nearest big box store and browsed the button-up shirt section. With a smile I chose two Hawaiian prints, tossed them into the cart and hurried to the check-out. In the parking lot I noticed how beautiful the day was growing. The sky was deep cerulean and adorned with happy, chubby clouds. There was a chill in the air that cut through the normally oppressive Georgia heat. Signs directing patrons to The Masters golf tournament were being hung in preparation, and that meant Augusta was painted with lush azaleas of every color. Bumblebees danced from flower to flower, and birds sang cheery songs of spring.

One stop at a drive-thru to grab a couple coffees and some breakfast sandwiches and I hurried back to the hotel. Liza was a great sleeper and hadn't even noticed I had left. I kissed her cheek to wake her.

"Happy wedding day babe, I got us breakfast…"

She shared a sleepy grin and sat up from her pillow, hair wild from a restful slumber. We sat close on the edge of the bed in the quietness of our room eating our fast food and sharing last minute nervous thoughts. We giggled and took selfies, one last date before we became old married folks. The whirlwind of the day swooped in and swallowed us up before we finished our coffees. Liza's sister Leah and my faithful Rosina joined us for hair, makeup, and mimosas. We donned our new Hawaiian shirts, a last minute purchase for two girls who didn't wear make up enough to know you needed button up shirts to get so fancy.

My face in the mirror changed as I transformed from regular old me to bride in waiting. All the make-up in the world couldn't have painted on the sparkle my eyes had been maintaining since I met Liza. It took a month of dating for me to tell her that I loved her over a pile of clean laundry as we folded it. It took a year for me to make the leap and move in with her and another year to officially propose to each other. We had spent the last year preparing the day we were about to experience.

It would be a lie to say planning a wedding was fun and easy. We agonized over our choices whether they were the choices everyone had to make like venue, food, flowers and cake; or whether they were uniquely lesbian decisions like who walks down the aisle first and what do we do with our dads? My biggest issue, perhaps not surprisingly, was what to do with God. Weddings are a sacred moment, you are literally promising before God and everyone to stay married forever. Figuring out how to fit him into the ceremony in a way that felt congruent with the state of my faith was so incredibly challenging.

Herein lies the problem for many of us. Spiritually, no matter your religion, is quite literally a lifelong journey. There are so many billions of questions to be asked and breath-takingly large puzzles to solve, but world religions reduce us to basic black and white closed ended trick questions and we feel a deep pressure to answer them with certainty. What do you make of Jesus!? Is he Lord, a liar or a lunatic? You can only pick one! We get squeezed into this pressure cooker feeling the obligation to give an answer and then be immediately embroiled with all the trappings that come from our decision. It makes sense, most religions are attempting to help us make sense of everything. I quite confidently believed I had all the answers at 18. It was so peaceful to be able to account for everything, to wipe the mystery and fear out of every potential situation.

What I truly longed to say about God, the way I most desired to incorporate him into not only my wedding but my entire life was to reserve the space to say "I don't know." That meant developing a tolerance for leaving the question-askers hanging even if I was the one asking. Not-knowing had to be okay. Curiosity was my spiritual practice. That's how I wanted God to show up in my wedding. He should be recognizable to everyone in the room regardless of the faith they practiced. I don't know anything with deep assurance. Will I love Liza for the rest of my life? That is my intention. Does God exist and waits to someday offer me entrance into Heaven? I hope so. What is Heaven? Got me. Every idea I've ever heard sounds mad boring. Better to not define and thereby not have to defend. Can't we just wait and be surprised?

The chairs arranged for our ceremony couldn't contain the

overflow of people who traveled hours to celebrate with us. We had both been afraid that no one would come. Running out of chairs soothed that fear and it gave birth to a new one about being in front of such a crowd. There were no bride or groom's sides of the aisle. All of our loved ones sat mingled in with one another: a symbol of how deeply intertwined our lives were becoming. My guests reflected every phase of my life. Family, childhood friends, and college friends had come. People traveled from Chicago, Charlotte and a half dozen friends from grad school, and the old cable company. I even received messages of joy and congratulations from friends all the way in Croatia.

As the music began, a hush fell over the crowd. Everyone stood and faced the center aisle, watching as Leah and Rosina walked in, both so beautiful. Liza's nephew carried in the rings. Everyone smiled and cooed at how handsome he was in his suit. We surprised everyone by walking in from opposite sides of the crowd and meeting in the center; a symbol of the journey we each had to make to find one another. From there we walked together toward the front where Julie was waiting to officiate. Liza and I declared our vows and read love letters to each other through giggles and tears. Longing to sing but absolutely unable to do so live, I prerecorded a Jennifer Knapp song to play as we passed our rings through the crowd asking guest to bless our love in accordance with their own faith. Julie invited us to seal our love with a kiss and with that, we were married.

The celebration that ensued after the ceremony was nothing short of epic. People still tell us ours was the best wedding they had ever attended. We walked in to our reception with RuPaul's "Sissy that Walk" playing over the speakers.

My cousins danced with my college friends. Laughter and reminiscing happened at every table. Everyone went back for seconds and thirds of our delicious food. Liza and I had our first dance to Kacey Musgrave's "Golden hour" and Rosina and Leah toasted us while we sipped very expensive champagne. The entire night was absolute perfection.

The next time I found a moment alone wouldn't be until the first morning of our honeymoon in Mexico. I sat in a hammock chair enjoying the breeze by our swim up balcony, sea birds calling in the distance. She was still asleep and I got on the wifi to check my social media. As I scrolled, my feeds were flooded with pictures from our wedding, everyone lavishing us with love and compliments. In no picture was there ever a grimace of disgust or a scowl of judgment, just joy and happiness.

Rocking in the hammock, I couldn't contain the tears flowing down my cheeks as I looked at the ring on my hand. I thought about every person who had paused to bless it; how significant they were to me; how much their opinions mattered. What specific blessing each person infused into our rings may always be a mystery, but it was clear to me that the singular wish of my heart, one I had blown into a magical little dandelion just a few years before, had come true that day. I had found my path. I found my place. In order to get there I had to find both myself and the courage to be that person. Only after I had been honest could I accept the most beautiful gift life could ever offer: everyone knew me completely and loved me still.